S.K. WEBB

a story of being both trapped by the bell,
and saved by it

TEACHERS
CRY TOO

Teachers Cry Too: a story of being both trapped by the bell, and saved by it
© S.K. Webb 2022

ISBN: 978-1-922644-73-2 (Paperback)
         978-1-922644-74-9 (eBook)

 A catalogue record for this book is available from the National Library of Australia

Editor: Kristy Martin
Cover Design: Ocean Reeve Publishing
Design and Typeset: Ocean Reeve Publishing
Printed in Australia by Ocean Reeve Publishing

Published by S.K. Webb and Ocean Reeve Publishing
www.oceanreevepublishing.com

DEDICATION

For all the students in my life,
And all the teachers in theirs.

DISCLAIMER

The stories in this book are representations of events and situations from different schools across a thirty-year career in education. Some names and identifying details have been disguised or omitted to protect the privacy of those involved, except for information that is on the public record, or where permissions have been obtained. Some characters are composites, and resemblance to individuals is coincidental.

This book deals with issues relating to mental health, including suicide and self-harm, and may contain triggering themes. The following organisations provide support for those who reside in Australia:

Lifeline 13 11 14
Kids Helpline 1800 551 800
Beyond Blue 1300 224 636
Headspace 1800 650 890
MensLine Australia 1300 789 978
ReachOut at au.reachout.com

This author has tried all reasonable means to contact all third-party sources. If any third party wish to discuss the use of their quotes or references in this book, please contact the author.

ACKNOWLEDGEMENTS

I owe a debt of gratitude to my earliest readers, who saw a story in what was little more than a journal. Thank you for the touchpoints throughout the process, which encouraged me to stick to my goal and see it through to completion. I am thankful to the trusted friends who listened patiently over endless cappuccinos and helped me workshop the ideas. You pressed me to name the truth and get the story right.

I am deeply thankful to those who generously gave me permission to share their stories too. Kindred spirits whose truth does not stand separate from my own.

If there is a hero that emerges in this story, it is James, who teaches me more about my strength than my weakness. You and the children are my reasons.

ACKNOWLEDGEMENT OF COUNTRY

I wish to acknowledge the Gubbi Gubbi (Kabi Kabi) people, the Traditional Custodians of the land upon which my story was lived and written. I pay respect to Elders past, present, and emerging.

INTRODUCTION

I've been a teacher for more than half my life. I've been a teacher for longer than I've been a wife and mother. I fell into teaching, really, after dropping out of an arts degree. But when I fell, I fell hard. I loved teaching from the very first day I stepped foot in a classroom and couldn't imagine wanting to do anything else. I landed in a career that ignited a passion, and as a young teacher, I felt blessed to be working alongside equally passionate teachers.

Teaching has brought me endless joy. But it has also brought its share of heartache. This is the reality of working with young people. I have stood in the glow of their achievements, and I've stood in the shadows of their despair. I have felt the intoxication of life overflowing and the agony of lives lost. I have been present at some of the most intimate moments of my students' lives, holding one young man as he collapsed into my arms the moment his father quietly passed away.

Teaching is a vocation of privilege. It is a window through which teachers witness other people's lives. Most are filled with love and opportunity, hope and optimism. But for too many, there is loneliness, sorrow, or violence. And these are the ones who need our time the most. Teaching is deeply emotional work. It is becoming even more so as schools seek to respond to a plethora of social crises—family and domestic violence, substance abuse, aggressive and antisocial behaviour, suicide rates, and the rising number of mental health issues affecting young people. Teaching is also deeply intense work. Teachers make hundreds of educational decisions a day, which can lead to decision fatigue—the brain is so exhausted and overloaded that it looks for shortcuts or stops working altogether.[1] My own experience has caused me to question how sustainable such intense work can be.

As I tried to keep up not only with the emotional demands of the job but also with the rapid changes to the profession, my work as a teacher became overwhelming. I found it difficult to separate my life as a wife and the mother of my own teenagers from the work I did with young people every day. The boundaries of my professional and personal life collided, so I could no longer see where one ended and the other began. Unfortunately, I didn't recognise the dangers of this until I spiralled into emotional collapse, by which time the damage had largely been done. I was reticent to acknowledge my illness for fear that in doing so, I might put at risk a career I loved and had dedicated half a lifetime to.

Almost half of all Australian adults meet the criteria for mental illness at some time in their lives.[2] This was my time. Although painful, in many ways, it has been the best teacher of all. This is not a story I wanted to write, but as it bled onto the pages of my journal, I realised it is a story that can be told a thousand times over. I pondered what was the better question: 'What happened?' or 'Why did it happen?' In writing it, I tried to pinpoint the events that led to my emotional collapse, hoping that I might offer my experience as a cautionary tale for others. I also hoped not only to find peace but that my story might contribute in a meaningful way to the important conversation of mental health.

I have tried to provide an insight into the day-to-day life of a teacher. Too often, teaching is reduced to headlines as the profession lobbies for better conditions. By and large, the public are well informed about what the challenges of teaching are—large class sizes, behavioural issues, an overcrowded curriculum, the need to support at-risk students, the occasional hostile advocacy from parents—to name a few. But to simply name these, even when they are supported by research, dilutes the impact of what this means for teachers as they navigate school life on a face-to-face basis.

The anecdotes in this book span a thirty-year teaching career, and I've done my best to tell the story authentically, knowing that memory is subject to the ebbs and flows of time. I offer it to anyone who has felt the crippling effects of mental illness. I offer it to all those who have a teacher in their lives. You will know that just like me, they cry too.

****

'Who is she?' they'll ask when they find an empty afternoon and time enough to pick up a book.

'Has she climbed a mountain?'

'Run a marathon?'

'Survived a war?'

She'll whisper a secret into a noisy world, a secret that reminds them truth doesn't always roar. They'll remember their own mountains, their own marathons, the battles from which they've emerged, survivors. They'll cry just a little bit. They'll smile knowingly and nod. They'll read about a woman they've met a thousand times over—somebody's mother, somebody's sister, somebody's wife, somebody's daughter, somebody's teacher, somebody's friend.

'Ah,' they'll say. 'She is just like me.'

CONTENTS

CHAPTER 1
THE EPISODE

Something's wrong. I blink away shadows that swim in the distance, blurring the road, and desperately try to remember where I'm heading.

'Mum, where are you going?' I hear Cate's voice from a long way away, dim despite being in the passenger seat beside me. Gripping the wheel, I try to make sense of the feeling of not really being there.

'Mum …' Her voice echoes faintly from somewhere close by, yet distant. Frantically, I fight to stay within my lane, which now floats groggily around me, making it hard to distinguish what's moving from what isn't.

Think, think, think! I tell myself urgently as I hurtle toward a head-on collision with my sanity; the car seems to have taken on a life of its own.

We need to get out. My words ricochet against the walls of a hidden sound tunnel; little word jabs catch me unaware and make me flinch. I drive directionless, searching for a familiar landmark but stuck in a mental loop I can't get off.

The outside world washes past, a watercolour highway of abstract colour without form. I have an overwhelming need to get out of the car to try to fend off the rising panic, or at least hide it from Cate.

Just pull over, for God's sake, and get out.

But the world moves in slow motion, trapping me in a Saturday morning time warp like a scene from a sci-fi movie, as though I've driven through an invisible void into a place in which time, sound, and gravity follow different rules.

When I eventually bring the car to a stop at an awkward angle outside the roadside café, it juts out like a broken bone, signalling a fractured state of mind. It's a freak abnormality among the other neatly parked cars lining the curb—misshapen and out of place.

You've made a dog's breakfast of that, girl! The words of my grandfather sit in judgement from beyond the grave. Struggling to make sense of the chaos in my head, I answer back, *If we were in Sicily, my car would be the rule, not the exception.* And partly because I knew Pop had never been to Sicily in his life, and partly because I was having an imaginary conversation with my dead grandfather—a grandfather I was not close to, a grandfather whose best friend was a stray dog named Dog—I wonder what on earth is wrong with me.

I shake my head to silence the voices and kickstart my thinking into normality, a gesture that would become quite common.

Once inside the café, I sink behind a booth, concealed somewhat by a dim amber light. Behind the counter, a milk steamer wails across the garbled conversations of other patrons. A bleary figure emerges and hovers patiently, waiting for our order. Cate asks for a hot chocolate, then elbows me for a response. 'Mum?'

'Cappuccino,' I murmur, pretending to look at the menu. When the drinks arrive, my hands shake, making it impossible to hug my coffee mug, a habit I'd formed as a first-year teacher in South Australia, where the chilly winter mornings numbed my fingers.

Instead, I place it on the table and stare as the chocolate powder clots onto the rim in sweet brown globs. I lift the cup to my lips and sip, waiting for the warm, creamy coffee to restore me, but it doesn't go down easily, and it doesn't make me feel better in the way it normally does. A film of wrinkly milk-skin forms as it goes cold, and despite the humidity, I feel a chill in the pit of my stomach.

****

This was what I've come to call 'the episode'. Driving my eleven-year-old daughter, Cate, to kayaking in October 2016, it came from nowhere, and I wasn't prepared. Despite regularly driving to Saturday morning sport, I had no idea where I was or where I was going. My brain and body had splintered and worked against each other, making it impossible to know where to go or how to get there.

Missing the exit wasn't new—I'd sailed straight past it a few weeks earlier while shouting answers at the radio during the Mad Minute. I'd done it again when Cate turned up the volume on her playlist, and we belted out the words to 'Bohemian Rhapsody', even before the film made the song famous for a new generation. In my defence, the lyrics are tricky. *'I see a little silhouetto of a man/ Scaramouche, Scaramouche, will you do the Fandango?'*

This was different. This was more than the eye-roll conversation that went along the lines of, 'Mum's missed the exit *again*.' On the day of the episode, I missed several of them without realising and couldn't get the car—or my head—back on track.

There we sat, Cate stirring sticky marshmallows into a milky drink, safely preoccupied while I teetered on the edge of a mental fragility that threatened to unravel my comfortable and ordered life. I use the word 'fragility' because, at that time, I didn't recognise myself as being unwell. It wouldn't be until much later I'd look back and be able to say the words 'mental illness'.

I assumed it would be a one-off incident and that after a coffee and some time to sit it out, I'd be fine. As it turned out, it took a lot more coffee and a lot longer than I anticipated. I don't remember driving home, but I must have because I locked myself in the bathroom, turned on the tap to drown out the noises hammering inside my head, and sobbed uncontrollably.

CHAPTER 2
A BLESSED LIFE

The screen door smacks. Instead of cursing it the way I usually do, I'm flooded with relief by its announcement that my husband is home. The acoustics of our Queenslander turn his home-from-work movements into a melody, like the kind I used to sing to the children when they were small—like 'A Teddy Bear's Picnic'.

> *Beneath the trees* … keys on the bench.
> *Where nobody sees* … fridge door open.
> *They'll hide and seek* … ginger beer pops.
> *As long as they please* … fridge door closes.
> *'Cause that's the way the teddy bears have their pic-nic.*

In my head, I hum a broken memory as James pulls off his beloved R.M. Williams boots and walks heavily through the house in his socks.

'Hi kids, where's Mum?' My head stops humming.

I'm in here, hiding and seeking and humming and crying, I want to call out, but the words get stuck in the teddy bear furball lodged in my throat. I've been crying all afternoon and don't know why. It's out of character for me. I'm edgy, distracted, and can't shake the sense of dread that descends like toxic smog.

He finds me hovering in the bathroom. I'd shut the door against the kids' inquisition, which I know would follow if they walked in and found me this way. They are not used to seeing me cry and wouldn't know what to do—how could they? How could I explain something to them that I don't understand myself? Through sobs, I tell James what happened, and I can tell he's worried. So am I. He asks me if anything is going on at school. *I can't think, I can't think.* Fuzzy thoughts sputter like the cheap toy walkie-talkies, which, for a few weeks, had turned our two children into would-be spies. Yes, I'm dealing with some mean-girls-on-Snapchat, but I'd dealt with many things like it before and felt it was in hand. Since taking on a coordinating role two years earlier, dealing with the fall out of teenage tug-of-war was almost a daily occurrence and something I took in my stride. But today, for some reason, I'm fearful and can't stop crying. James puts his arms around me and says quietly, 'We've got this.' I cling to the word 'we'.

****

James and I met in October 1998 while we were teaching together in Central Queensland. He was twenty-three and had just returned from a summer sojourn in the United Kingdom. He'd secured a housemaster's position at a nearby boarding school, which enabled him to live on campus, and had picked up a short-term teaching contract at the same school in which I was working. I'd relocated from Adelaide to take up a position as the head of the English faculty. There is a nine-year age difference between us, and at thirty-two, I had some misgivings when we first met. Things are changing these days, but back then it was not commonplace for a woman to date a man nine years her junior. However, as our relationship grew, it became less of an issue. One we mostly felt—and laughed about—in our choice of music.

Being a teacher was thrilling. No two days were the same, and I couldn't believe my luck at being paid to do a job I couldn't wait to get to each morning. It was a large school by Catholic standards, and I cut my teeth on leadership opportunities more often afforded to teachers in regional communities. It was here, in Rockhampton, where I learned about my craft, established my career, and fell in love.

Our weekends consisted of day trips to Great Keppel Island, one of a group of islands known as 'the Keppels' that dot the Coral Sea, just north of the Tropic of Capricorn. The ferry to the island departed from Rosslyn Bay Harbour, and as it pulled away from the wharf, we sat up on deck feeling the breeze on our faces, squinting as the sun reflected off a boundless oceanic playground. The island's powdery white beaches grew larger with our approach, and after disembarking, we joined scores of day-trippers swimming and floating lazily in the tropical waters. When the sun went down, gradually yielding its strength, the night air cooled our sunburnt skin and promised the joys that evenings bring when you're young and time seems to stretch out forever.

At that time, the advertising campaign for the island was Get Wrecked on Keppel, and occasionally we did, at events like the Bachelor and Spinsters Ball, a four-day event that kicked off in Rockhampton, locally known as The Rocky B and S. There were some memorable New Year's Eve parties drinking Midori and champagne by the jug and dancing under a vast sky until dawn cast a subdued hue over the ocean, reminding me that an exciting new day filled with endless possibilities was coming. It felt like the island separated us from the rest of the world, as islands do, and allowed us, for a time, to bask in our little paradise.

Sometimes after school, we drove the forty kilometres from Rockhampton to Yeppoon, a seaside town known as the southern gateway to the Great Barrier Reef, where we enjoyed romantic dinners away from the students in our classes, who we inevitably bumped into closer to home. We joined the small army of other young teachers discovering the fun there is to be had in regional towns where we largely had to make our own. One of the great things about teaching is that schools are ready-made communities within themselves, and we have many fond memories of forging the friendships we still enjoy to this day.

When a group of us splurged on a long weekend at Laguna Quays, a resort near Mackay, I had a go at windsurfing, something I'd wanted to try for a long time. The rest of the crew stood on the foreshore taking it in turns to shout instructions as I battled the wind, the force of which nearly ripped my arms off when it caught the sail.

'Stick ya bum in,' one of the guys boomed, hands cupped around his mouth. Macca had grown up surfing and made it look easy.

'Stick it in the other way,' he yelled out seconds later, which made me laugh and lose my balance completely. I swallowed half the ocean as I went under. I resurfaced to hear them clapping theatrically at my calamitous attempt and looked around to find the board had capsized, the sail floating like a soggy pancake behind me.

There were endless rounds of barbecues, weekends away, and social games of mixed netball and beach volleyball. On Saturdays, James played rugby for Central Queensland University, and on game nights, we joined most of the population between the ages of eighteen-ish and thirty-five in a mass migration from the Criterion Hotel to a nightclub called the Pink Flamingo, which stayed open until 3 am. I say 'ish' because we'd sometimes see our students at the bar as well. There seemed to be a casual understanding that this was life in the beef capital of Australia—*The place where the Outback meets the Coast.*

Most Friday afternoons, after the whirring of the photocopiers ground to a halt and piles of marking had been snatched up from our too-small carrels, we'd call out to anyone still left in the staffroom, 'Seeya at the Cri.' Built in 1889, the Criterion Hotel sits on the corner of Quay and Fitzroy Streets, and I loved its character. It reminded me of the pub my grandparents took me to as a kid in Adelaide, where they bought me raspberry lemonade or, as a special treat, a spider. I'd watch in anticipation as the ice cream made the icy cold drink fizz up like it was alive, spilling over the edge so that I had to lick the glass to catch the spider's legs as they dripped down the side.

I didn't grow up with my grandparents and never knew them well, but if we visited on pension days, Pop dug into the pocket of his trousers with tobacco-stained fingers and found twenty-cent pieces to put in the beer slot. He spoke gruffly, his years on the road as a swaggie having sloughed off the edges of sentimentality.

'Here, girl. See whatcha can do with that.' The silver coins clinked as the machine swallowed them up and spat out a ticket.

'You bloody bewdy,' he'd say when it was a winner. This meant he could call past the bottle shop on the way home to claim his beloved Coopers beer, which he carried down the street in a brown paper bag. Nan drank Coopers too, and always a lady, she sipped delicately from a small glass called a 'pony'. When they were in the grip of an oppressive Adelaide heatwave, she'd order a shandy, and if I nagged for long enough, she'd give in and let me have a sip. Sometimes, the 'rabbit man' would come through the old Kilburn Hotel, and she'd buy a rabbit wrapped in newspaper to make rabbit stew.

These are some of the handful of memories I have of my grandparents, and when I walked into the Criterion, I was reminded of my visits with them in childhood—simple days drinking spiders, sucking on defiant yellow soursobs that menaced their veggie patch, and eating rabbit stew.

As well as weekend trips to the beach, we occasionally went to see live bands play in the various pubs around town. During end-of-term holidays, we drove out to the now-abandoned Capricorn International Resort, which at the time boasted the largest outdoor swimming pool in the Southern Hemisphere. These were easy years, filled with the spontaneity of being young, having a regular cash flow, and free weekends in which to spend it.

Most nights after he'd knocked off in the boarding house, James came around to my small but comfortable—and most importantly in the constant humidity—air-conditioned unit, where we talked until the early hours of the morning and dreamed of our future. While I'd had previous relationships, one that was serious and long term, James had a steadiness that set him apart. He was fun and careful at the same time. Younger than me but, perhaps because of his country upbringing, more grounded.

I'd chosen the job in Rockhampton over teaching positions in the United Arab Emirates and joked about the irony of finding my prince in Central Queensland. We tried to be discreet about our relationship because romances between staff were a topic of wild speculation among students, and I knew we'd be watched with interest; in 'Rock Vegas' however, where the senior students were often in the same pubs and clubs we were, our relationship was the worst-kept secret in the school.

Like many teachers who time their lives around school terms and holiday periods, we were married in December 2000. It was the turn of a new century and the beginning of adult life for us, which happened in quick succession when I fell pregnant with our son and we took out our first mortgage.

Michael was born in 2002, and even before he took his first breath, he was the centre of our lives. By then I'd accepted an assistant principal's position on the Gold Coast, where James managed to secure a job as a primary school physical education (PE) teacher.

When Michael arrived, I took one year's maternity leave, and James took the following year off to be 'Mr Mum', a decision driven by the fact that I was earning more than he was, and we were relying too much on credit. I fretted about leaving my baby, and my first day back at work seemed interminably long as I transitioned away from feed times and back to the rhythm of school life with its fifty-minute bell times. When I got home at the end of my first day back, James greeted me at the door with a clean baby on his hip and held out a glass of wine with a grin that said, 'See, I told you I could do it!' I laughed and had to admit he'd done better than I'd expected, although there was no sign of dinner.

While most nights I'd managed to have a meal simmering on the hob, I usually welcomed James home with Mike's dummy clenched between my teeth and a nappy flung over my shoulder to catch the baby sick after his five o'clock feed. That night, we ordered takeaway from our local Indian restaurant, and as I dipped the cheesy garlic naan into my lamb korma, I relaxed with the realisation that James would be a different stay-at-home parent than me, but I liked things the way he did them too.

Together, father and son became adventurers, exploring rockpools on the beach and bringing home little treasures they'd found half-buried in the sand. One day, they called in to the Kurrawa Surf Club for lunch and hit the jackpot, winning $600 on Keno. James waved the cash in front of him, gloating about earning more than me that day.

His adjustment to being the primary carer wasn't all smooth sailing, though, and one afternoon, he rang me at work.

'Now, I don't want you to panic,' he said, the worst way to start a conversation with a new mother who's left her baby.

'What? What's happened?' My stomach lurched.

'I've put Michael's head in the fan.'

'What! Oh my God, where is he?' I pictured the circular whirring of the blades on the overhead fan in our lounge room and closed my eyes against the horrific images of my baby's dented and deformed skull.

'I'm on my way to the doctor now. He didn't cry much. There's no blood …' I heard the fright and the forced restraint in his voice as he tried, for my sake, to sound calmer than he was.

'I'll meet you there.'

I raced to meet them at the clinic and rushed into the examination room to find James mid-explanation. He'd been feeding the baby in his highchair, which he'd placed in front of the television so he could watch the cricket. Just as he was lifting Michael out, Australia took a wicket, and with a jubilant 'Howzat!' he tossed him high into the air and straight into the overhead fan. Thankfully, he bounced right off it, and the nurse cleared him of injury, but to this day, if someone accuses him of not thinking quickly enough, Mike says, 'I blame Dad.'

As he got older, the two of them became great mates. They shared lots of common interests: their love of cricket, road trips, watching the footy, camping. Surrounded by the mantra that *camping is good for kids,* I'd tried hard to like it, but when a giant goanna sprinted across our tent one night, it was the last nail in my camping coffin. I lay awake in the darkness of the Amamoor State Forest, praying that our Kmart tent was sturdy enough to withstand the nocturnal wildlife that rustled all around us, deciding then and there my camping days were over.

Many of our friends shared fond memories of outdoor adventures in places like Rainbow Beach and Double Island Point, but I never got used to sleeping rough. I hated the smell of campfire smoke in my clothes, loathed the mosquito bites, the ants, and the dirt, which always made its way into my sleeping bag no matter how careful I was. In my opinion, sleeping under the stars sounds a lot more comfortable than it actually is. Despite accusations of being un-Australian, I'm not a fun camper, and although I quite like the idea of it, I've never learned to embrace the reality of it. Instead, I looked for other ways to stay connected with my young son.

When he was eleven, we went to watch the Ashes test cricket series in Adelaide. At the time, most of our afternoons at home were punctuated by the summertime thuds of batting practice. This consisted of a cricket ball in a stocking tied to a beam on the open verandah. Mike refined his batting technique: left elbow high in the air, hitting the ball back and forward, back and forward. There were days when the *thock, thock, thock* of batting practice drove me bonkers, but when he stopped playing cricket in senior high school, I missed the sound of leather on willow and the echo it sent across our yard.

We sat together at the Adelaide Oval in the summer of 2013 on seats close enough to touch the fence, and we felt like we were part of the action. Fast bowler Mitchell Johnson was on fire; he took 7 for 40 and became the hero of the series, which was a five-nil whitewash. We clapped slowly when he began his run-up and built into a crescendo as he approached the crease. Michael knew every player, told me their stats, explained some of the finer rules of the game and terms like 'googly' and 'silly mid-off'. When the crowd booed Stuart Broad and I shifted uncomfortably in my seat, he explained the context. Then the crowd roared when Broad was bowled out for a duck after he delayed play to adjust the sightscreen.

At the end of the day's play, I gave Mike the map of the CBD and said, 'You choose somewhere for dinner and then work out how to get us there.' We walked with the crowds from the Adelaide Oval to Victoria Square, where he navigated the trams and buses around the inner city and chose from one of the many trendy restaurants and cafés that now define Adelaide. He practised finding the way back to our hotel, which he did with remarkable ease. Years later, on a ski trip to Japan, Michael nailed the complexity of the Japanese rail system with its colour-coded urban and intercity lines, finding his way around the imposing Japanese railway stations like a pro.

Our daughter, Cate, was born in 2004, and in the same year, James swapped teaching for the corporate world of the pharmaceutical industry. He was offered a promotion in 2006, which meant relocating to the Sunshine Coast. My experience in leadership roles stood me in good stead, and it didn't take long to find a teaching position. We didn't have any family close by, so we pieced together the childcare jigsaw by reducing our working week, each taking a day off to be with the children. James chose not to work on Fridays, and when Michael started school, Cate had her dad all to herself. It was hard to tell which of them was more excited as they headed off for day-long adventures to Queensland Zoo, a small children's petting zoo situated at the iconic Big Pineapple. They fed barnyard animals and rode the small train as it chugged through a bamboo forest. They climbed the volcanic peak of Mount Coolum and always sent me a pic from the top with the view of the coastline far below, stretching from Double Island Point to Caloundra.

They spent hours in our backyard pool, James throwing Cate around like a rag doll and encouraging her to jump off the edge and dog paddle to the side so she could get herself out if she fell in. I'd come home in the afternoon and insist she'd had enough, her lips blue and quivering with cold. Inevitably she resisted, calling for more and jumping off before he was there to catch her. I sometimes watched with my heart in my mouth as she sank towards the bottom of the pool, her blonde baby hair swishing beneath the surface before she bobbed up, gurgling, giggling, even while spurting water out of her mouth. She could kick her way to the pool's edge before she could walk. James would hand her up to me, and I'd wrap her in a dry towel, cocoon-like, chubby legs dangling, and plonk her into a warm bath to thaw out.

Thursdays with Cate, our day at home together, unfolded organically. They were often spent on the lounge room floor, buried beneath the hordes of books we borrowed from the children's library, playing word games and making up stories. We baked chocolate brownies and choc chunk cookies, which have become her specialty, and even now are in constant demand from the boys. She trotted along beside me when I joined the other mums visiting Michael's prep and grade one classrooms, listening as the kids sounded their way through First Readers, unaware that in doing so, they became her first teachers.

As she approached her adolescent years, Cate fell into stride beside me, usually with her arm looped through mine or unselfconsciously holding my hand as she told me about the stories of her day. I suspected that while they were grounded in fact, they were peppered with just enough fiction to make them as entertaining as she found her life to be. She was a joyful kid, skipping and cartwheeling her way through primary school and embracing each new phase of growing up with the same give-it-a-go confidence with which she approached the highest and wildest rides she inevitably chose when we went to the Ekka, Brisbane's annual show.

Many times, James and I have taken it in turns to swallow our nausea as Cate wanted to go higher, further, faster, but wasn't tall enough to ride without a parent. She's the only one in our family brave enough to bungee jump, and my mum, always bemused by her antics, has remarked more than once, 'That child spends half her life upside down.' I can't help but wonder whether it's because of this she has an ability to consider life from different perspectives.

When she was about twelve, I finally relented and gave in to her pleas to watch the American teen drama *Gossip Girl* that 'everyone else' had seen and was talking about at school. We watched it together and popcorned our way through the complete series of spoiled rich kids living impossible lives on Manhattan's Upper East Side. We pinkie-promised not to watch an episode without each other, rehashing the clues and hypothesising in our efforts to solve the mystery of who *was* the elusive Gossip Girl? We spent the entire mid-year school holidays in our lounge room, having hijacked the television and shooed the boys out to watch the footy somewhere else, ruthlessly judging Serena and Blair in their selfishness, binge-watching every juicy minute of it.

When Cate started her first casual job at our local McDonald's, true to form, she came home from her shifts with a story to tell, relaying hilarious anecdotes about eccentric customers or the crisis of a broken ice cream machine on a forty-degree day. She shook her head at the impossibility of persuading the oldies to order through the self-serve kiosk instead of at the register. 'It's a lost cause, Mum,' she'd say, and when I encouraged her not to give up so easily, suggesting that her job was not to sell cheeseburgers and frozen cokes that sold themselves, but to sell the self-serve kiosk instead, she took it on as a personal mission. Sometimes she came home and said, 'I had such a great shift, Mum,' then she'd fling off her apron, toss her work-issued cap on the bed, and entertain us for the next fifteen minutes with the frantic but fun goings-on behind the scenes of rush hour at the Macca's drive-thru.

Although James has remained in the corporate sector and has chosen not to return to education, he is a natural teacher and mentor for young people. Being familiar with the world of teaching, he remains my go-to person, my confidante when there are tricky and sensitive issues to work through at school. At home, although we might come up with different ways to navigate family life—he is spontaneous, with an easy sense of humour, while I am more routine driven—I'd always felt that we were a good team. Before the 'episode', I had a marriage I was proud of and lived on the coast, where it's warm all year round. Life wasn't always perfect, but it was usually pretty close to it. I'd been christened 'The Blessed One' by an aunty because of it. Life was busy, sometimes hectic, but it was filled with 'good times', as Michael put it.

Like all parents, we celebrated the joy in simple moments—watching our children become young adults, sharing banter around the dinner table, walking along the beach, barbecues with friends.

Our home life was typical of a family, filled with school runs, weekend sport, mid-week training, homework, and the occasional holiday when the term came to an end. Like all working mums, there were days when I felt I had too many balls in the air, and occasionally I dropped a few. However, until that moment driving along the Sunshine Motorway on a completely normal Saturday morning, I'd never experienced the terrifying chaos that happens when your mind snaps.

And then I did.

CHAPTER 3
A FAULTY RADAR

I want this horrible-never-ending-mind-cracking-manic day to be over. All I want to do is curl up on the bed and make the world stop spinning, to vomit this emotional hangover out of my system. James tells me he's rung the assistant principal to say I won't be coming in tomorrow. He's in management mode, and this is him stepping in. I panic. Frantically I question him about how he's explained my absence. He reassures me he hasn't given anything away, but he's making an appointment with our GP tomorrow, and he's coming with me.

'No. I'll go by myself.' I try to sound convincing.

'No, I'm coming with you,' he says firmly. James is almost never bossy, but this afternoon he's adamant, and he won't be negotiated out of it. *Shit.* Now I'm going to have to have a conversation, and it will need to be coherent. Somebody else is going to know, and I am so embarrassed. Taking a day off means that I must go in to school to set work for tomorrow's classes, postpone a meeting, and reschedule an appointment with a parent who's coming in. Even though it's Sunday, I know there will be other teachers at school getting organised for the coming week, and I don't want to cross paths with my colleagues. I drag myself out of bed, pull on a pair of jeans, and tie my hair back into something I hope looks passable. I hide in my office and try to fill in the teacher-relief sheets, but it's slow going because my thoughts are jumping all over the place, and I don't know if any of it makes sense. My tears blot the pages.

****

As James and I sat in the GP's office the next day, I was determined to be the measured and professional Monday morning person I used to be. I'd practised my words and calmly described the incident that had taken place two days earlier.

'I feel much better,' I lied, explaining that as we drew closer to the end of the school year, there were events on the calendar for which I was responsible, and I didn't want to miss them. I'd made James promise to let me do the talking, and he'd made me promise to take time off—extended time off—if the doctor suggested it. I dreaded having to tell my principal that I needed time off work because unexpected sick leave would not only draw more attention than I was ready for, but it would also have a knock-on effect.

Teacher absences, and the reason for their absence (illness, long-service leave, professional development), were distributed to staff via a bulletin so we knew whose classes needed to be covered. In addition, extended leave, even for a week, would require a staffing reshuffle to cover my role as coordinator and an official communique to the parents of the year level for which I was responsible. Knowing the way schools work, knowing the protocols that needed to be followed, I was gripped by shame at the prospect that my sick leave would become public knowledge. Everyone would know.

The idea of having to ask for leave—stress leave—made me feel sicker than I did already, and I concentrated hard as I answered the doctor's questions. Over the weekend, James and I had been at a loss as to what might be causing my distress, and I knew he was listening for a cue from the doctor. However, if it came, I was worried about losing my sense of agency. It was one thing for me to call in sick, a choice I was in full control of, but it was another thing altogether to put myself in a position where somebody else—my husband, my doctor, my employer—might decide this on my behalf. I concentrated hard and pleaded with the universe, *Don'tsayit, Don'tsayit, Don'tsayit*.

The universe listened, the voices inside my head listened, and the doctor listened. Then he said, 'Panic attack.' He said he'd never heard anyone articulate their experience with such clarity. This was ironic, but not surprising—it had played repeatedly in my head, and I'd prepared for this appointment like it was a job interview. I'd learned my lines as if rehearsing for an audition, believing that if I was convincing enough, I could simply resume my usual role. I reassured him I would come back if things got worse, then flew out of there, relieved the doctor hadn't thought I was losing it. A panic attack was a one-off thing, right? It was a finite, tangible thing. A singular noun. James didn't say much, but I could tell he wasn't sold.

As soon as I walked through the door, I emailed the assistant principal. *There's a girl I'm worried about—do you mind going to her classroom and letting me know if she's at school today?* I didn't want to rely on the attendance record, which can sometimes be wrong, and hoped he would go and check for himself.

Yes, his reply came, *She's here, and she seems fine.*

I was still worried, though, because the girl's mother had shared some concerns.

I emailed the school counsellor and asked her to see the student as a matter of priority. What if I'd missed something? All afternoon, I checked my emails obsessively for a response from the counsellor, which, when it came, should have reassured me, but it didn't.

Going straight back into work mode was a welcome distraction from the turmoil I felt and an attempt to reassure myself that I was still in control. If I pretended hard enough that everything was normal, I could make it so. *Fake it until you make it,* I told myself. But the professional responsibility I usually carried as I went about school life—the duty of care I'd internalised early in my career—suddenly seemed heavier than it had before.

James came quietly into the room with a cup of tea.

'You're supposed to be having a day off,' he said. 'Get off your email.'

****

I went into school on Tuesday feeling like I'd been on a three-day bender. Not that I'd ever had one, but I once shared a flat with a girl who had them regularly enough for me to know the signs. I was ragged. I'd hardly slept or eaten since Saturday; I had a raging headache and felt like I wanted to throw up. Some of my colleagues asked me if I was feeling better, and I said, 'Yes, thank you.' It was a polite, almost rhetorical exchange that didn't require a truthful answer. Like when you pass someone in the street and say, 'Hey, how's it going?' Everybody knows a brief, 'Good, thanks,' and a nod completes the transaction.

Grateful that nobody probed further, I walked along the staffroom corridor, which seemed longer than it had on Friday. I edged the wall in case I needed to reach out to steady myself. I felt off balance and otherworldly—like I was there, but not there.

Holding my breath against the haze of body spray around the boys' lockers, I unlocked the classroom, and the students spilled through the door. In high school, they don't line up in front of the teacher like they do in primary school. They hover. Like bees.

True to form, students swarmed in with gossip about who said what to whom on group chats from the night before. Latecomers sauntered reluctantly through the door. One girl had a look of thunder. Something had happened on the bus. Something usually happens on the bus. Different versions of the event were thrown around until they moved on to another topic. The thrum of the classroom washed over me, and I hid among it because mercifully, I wasn't expected to contribute much to this early morning banter.

A junior student bobbed along beside me as I headed to my next lesson, her ponytail flicking as she half walked, half skipped into her day. She talked non-stop, happily chatting away, and then stopped, waiting expectantly. I looked back at her blankly.

'So, can I, Miss?'

She was waiting for an answer, but I had no awareness of anything she'd said. No clue. Nothing. After a few seconds of awkward silence, I tried to make a joke and asked her to repeat the question.

'Sorry,' I laughed, a bit too loudly. 'I haven't had my morning coffee yet.'

Years in the classroom have trained me to be attentive when kids talk, to scan the conversation carefully. A wobbly word, a too-light tone, an almost imperceptible hesitation—all are clues to what a student might be trying to tell you. I've learned to listen just as intently for what isn't said because what a child leaves out or avoids can say just as much as the conversation itself.

My radar pinged over breakfast one morning when James and I were watching *The Today Show*, which at the time was co-hosted by Lisa Wilkinson. James was thumbing through the paper, as always, starting at the back with the sports section. The telly played in the background, and as we ate breakfast, I looked up suddenly to pay closer attention. I sipped my coffee and watched more intently, trying to work out what had caught my ear.

'Something's up with Lisa,' I said out loud, but more to myself than to him.

'What do you mean?' James glanced up from the paper, munching on his toast.

'I don't know.' I frowned. 'I just think something's not right.' There was nothing in her script or in the usual line-up of the show that suggested something wasn't right, but there was a different tone, a subtle, restrained tension in her voice, a casualness she was trying too hard for. Later in the broadcast, she explained that she'd been worried about her son who was in Berlin when a truck ploughed through the Christmas markets in a suspected terror attack. Nobody had been able to contact him, and she'd had to cover the story not knowing whether he was safe or not. James looked from the television to me and said, 'How'd you pick that?'

It's not like I know Lisa Wilkinson personally, or even that we watched breakfast television all that often. It's just that years of listening intently to students, listening to what they're trying to say but don't yet have the words for, had trained me to home in, to take note when something was amiss.

So as my junior student stood patiently waiting for the answer to a question I hadn't even heard, I was unsettled because I knew this deafness wasn't like me. Thankfully, she bounced along without missing a beat and simply asked me again. But I was left with a niggling feeling that something wasn't quite right and the uncomfortable suspicion that my radar was on the blink.

CHAPTER 4
CHAOS

Night terrors kick me out of bed at 2 am after an almost impossible week. My side is a crumpled, chaotic mess, a war of bed linen that looks even more dishevelled next to James's sleeping stillness. Anything is preferable to the fear that sits in my throat whenever I close my eyes, so I wander restlessly, making my way for the third time towards the children's bedrooms. A slight movement from outside catches my eye, and I stop and pull back the curtains to peer searchingly into the darkness. A single streetlight illuminates the huge paperbark at the front of our yard. Drooping from the ongoing drought, its branches bend to the pre-summer winds that swoop the house and cast slinking shadows in the moonlight. Goaded by night-time devilry, the house contracts in the night air and creaks back. Like co-conspirators, they work together. *It's not fair*, I think. *It's two against one.* But they've smelled the fear.

****

Normally, I loved the way our Queenslander talked to us as it breathed with the seasons like it was part of the family. When lightning shows tore the sky during torrential summer storms, we sheltered in front-row seats on the wide verandah, yelling above nature's thunderous applause. On warm, quiet evenings, the piercing call of a koel bird beckoned us outside to watch crimson brush the sky. We sat on the wooden steps, drinking in the eucalypts while night descended and streetlights strung houses together like lantern bunting. But that Friday night, and on the nights that followed, each sound was a warning, and I shuddered as I felt the reality of the witching hour. As I stood at the window, my body swayed involuntarily, the way mothers do even when their children have grown too heavy for their hip. Daylight cracked, coating the world in monochrome, and I went to lie down again beside James, drifting in and out of fitful sleep.

Most mornings, I woke pressed with an unnamed burden, restlessness driving me out of the house just after dawn. It took a herculean effort to put one foot in front of the other, and my breathing was out of sync as I wrestled with time that fractured around me.

Usually, an early morning walk kicked off my planning for the day ahead, thoughts slotting into mental files as I fine-tuned meeting proposals and composed emails. By the time my fitness app showed a healthy 5,000, give or take, I had a blueprint for how I wanted things to unfold. But in the weeks following the panic attack, my feet stumbled over themselves, and my thinking was scrambled. I couldn't find a rhythm when I walked along the beach. I trod too heavily, sank too deeply into the sand. Sunglasses did little to shield me from the glaring, staring outside world.

I walked past the local skate park at Alexandra Headland where students sometimes hung out before school. Young Evel Knievels balanced on the deck of the half-pipe and pushed off into a vertical drop. If they were good enough, they flew down the side, rolled into the bowl, and made it all the way back up the other side. If they weren't, they bailed out, and the skateboard shot out from beneath them. Some mornings, they called out to me as I walked past, and I'd stop and watch for a while. But not then. Then I prayed I wouldn't bump into anyone I knew because I couldn't talk to them and deal with the voices in my head at the same time.

At least the voices I'm hearing now are my own, I thought wryly, and there was some fleeting comfort because surely a sense of humour and an inkling of self-awareness meant I wasn't completely nuts. Yet.

In the first few weeks of my illness, the physical manifestations were both overwhelming and inescapable. I was jumpy and shook my head to short circuit the constant reruns that played over and over and over until they became so firmly lodged, they consumed me. My love of American crime shows like *CSI* and *Law and Order: SVU* had planted images in my mind of manic street people marooned beneath bridges, vagrant and discarded, cast adrift by addled minds. They smacked themselves in the head or shuffled from foot to foot in constant agitation, the need to move their bodies something I now recognised. As self-assured detectives questioned these city drifters, they repeated themselves with rambling incoherence in scenes that were both comical and tragic. *Please, God, don't let me drift too far,* I thought. The distance between shaking my head and hitting it, between pacing from room to room and shuffling from foot to foot, felt far too short.

The need to appear anchored in my professional life became all-consuming. I planned and revised every communication—every email, every text message, every adjustment to every student record. When phone conversations were unavoidable, I made sure I had a script to rely on because I had to work so hard at being articulate. Off-the-cuff banter became a thing of the past as I floundered among the noise overload at school. Mouthfuls of blurry words came at me, muffled like the mournful drone of a song played at slow speed. I frowned as sentence fragments swirled and gurgled, clogging my thoughts. Once just white noise against the background of school life, the crows outside my classroom screeched mercilessly, tugging at lunch bag leftovers, a stark warning of the way predators make short work of the scrap heap. I photocopied class sets of work activities, only to find I'd already done it and the bundles sat, ready to be distributed, on my desk.

My inability to make sense of and retain information was a big problem for me at school, where teachers are swamped with detail, sometimes of a confidential and sensitive nature. Now that I struggled to remember simple things, like the names of new staff, I had to find workarounds for the blank gaps that got in the way of doing my job. Meeting agendas became useful props not because of the neatly dot-pointed agenda items but because at the top of the page was the list of attendees—often the very same people I'd been working with all day.

Even a simple timetable change sent me spinning. The puzzled look on a colleague's face when I kept walking in on her senior maths class for weeks after a classroom swap told me I was testing her patience. She was always too polite to say so, but I knew losing the flow of a lesson because of unnecessary interruptions was exasperating. It also meant I was late for my class, which was left standing outside an empty classroom waiting for me to get from one side of the school to the other. My teacher diary became an indispensable record of every tiny reminder, and misplacing it meant forgetting a yard duty or being a no-show for a meeting. Schools tend to be unforgiving when it comes to missing yard duty, as we can be held liable for accidents or injuries. The schoolyard at lunchtime is also where bullying is more likely to take place, and although the duty is only twenty minutes or so, a lot can happen in that time without an adult around.

Now that I could no longer rely on my memory, I carried a pen wherever I went in case I was given information on the hop and needed to jot it down, often on the back of my hand. Retractable pens with click tops were the best because the sound of the small click when I pushed the nib in and out helped keep me focused—no doubt an annoying habit for anyone who worked nearby. The tactile nature of holding a pen has become a lasting habit. Even when I'm working on a computer, there is always a pen within reach—held in my hand for proofreading and usually clamped between my teeth when editing.

I was also vague at home, perhaps even more so because the need for pretence wasn't as great. James looked at me sometimes with an expression that said, 'We've already had this conversation, don't you remember?' I knew the look. It was the one people try to mask when they meet someone and they're politely trying to work out just how not-quite-right in the head they are. My not-quite-rightness varied daily and presented practical inconveniences like finding a forgotten load of washing clumped in the bottom of the machine. It meant the everyday jobs I hadn't got around to needed explaining. One day, Michael, then fourteen, bought a laundry basket for his room and began to do his own washing so he had clean uniforms for school the next day.

In different circumstances, I might have taken pride in the fact that my adolescent son knew how to do his own laundry. But each time he went out to the clothesline, I felt my failure and the fear of drifting further away. Paradoxically, the smell of freshly washed bed sheets became a comforting symbol of my safe middle-class stability, and I washed the linen obsessively. A clean bed each night, even one I had trouble falling asleep in, enabled me to cling to a measure of security.

Was I simply experiencing the side-effects of a panic attack, or was there something more sinister at play? It was becoming apparent that my symptoms were escalating, but the more I lost control, the more desperate I became to make it appear otherwise.

Disregarding the dangers of self-diagnosis, I attempted to do just that. This approach was careless and not one I would recommend. Dr Google presented a gamut of possibilities: anxiety, depression, stress, burnout, post-traumatic stress disorder, or perhaps a combination of these. I continued to dodge a more serious diagnosis, one that might require prolonged treatment and possibly medications that might take weeks to get right. This meant that strategies to mask my state of mind became important.

To avoid the subtleties of social interaction, and so I didn't get drawn into the minutiae of small talk, I avoided making eye contact with people and emitted 'don't-come-near-me' vibes like a walking sonar. This reduced my risk of getting drawn into plans I knew I wouldn't be able to keep. On the rare occasions when James and I still went out socially, I gravitated gratefully toward older folk, many of whom tend to be storytellers rather than conversationalists. Their tales, slow-moving stories told in soothing timbres, carried me temporarily into their lives and away from my own. This was just one of many strategies I developed to circumvent the embarrassing moments when I got people's names wrong or didn't remember who I'd already been introduced to.

On the way to events, I constructed mental name charts and went through them like a roll call, hoping to commit them to memory by rote. I hovered on the outskirts of James's conversations, during which he'd discreetly drop a name to cue me, and this at least helped me to minimise, although not altogether avoid, embarrassing social gaffes.

It was easier to pull off when we attended his social functions because while it's not ideal, it is at least excusable to forget the names of the people in your partner's circle.

When I couldn't remember the names of my own people, some of them who'd been at the school for a long time and with whom I interacted daily, I felt exposed by social ineptitude. In these situations, James became adept at jumping in to introduce himself when he sensed any hesitation from me.

'G'day, I'm James—Sue's husband,' he'd say, leaning in casually to shake hands. His affable meet-and-greet was enough to deflect attention away from me and earned him a reputation among my colleagues as being friendly and outgoing. As an extrovert, this is his natural disposition, and I relied on it to buy me time until I could converse at a level that wouldn't arouse suspicion.

I dodged the grocery shopping, a milieu of social small talk and multitasking. Shopping of any sort can be tricky for teachers because we work with upwards of 150 students a day, many of whom have after-school or weekend jobs, so we rarely just pop in and out. Although the spouses of my teacher friends bemoan shopping because it takes a lifetime to get from one end of the mall to the other, I had always enjoyed this connection to my community. However, now I was no longer capable of the friendly conversation I usually engaged in; I was flat out following the shopping list and didn't dare risk the pitfalls of casual chit-chat that might give me away.

For the most part, the strategising, the planning, and the avoidance were enough to make it appear I was going about daily life as I always had. But no matter how hard I tried, nothing could stop the horrible images that made their way in and out of my thoughts whenever I was alone. If I read about an assault, a house fire, or a car fatality, I obsessed over the possibility that it could be me, my children, or my husband. I made up scenarios and played them out in my mind. I felt every bad news story, every tragedy, every accident as if I were living through it. My imaginings became as real as the breaking news stories that fed them. I heard the roaring flames of our house on fire and imagined the kids trapped by a fantasy inferno. The graphic news footage I watched each night was fodder for my already out-of-control imagination, which was the only part of my mind that didn't have to work hard at all.

Had the imaginings remained just that, they may have assumed the same status in my mind as nightmares we can shrug off. However, my imaginings led to obsessive and troubling behaviour. I put rocks outside the kids' bedroom windows in case I needed to smash my way through to them in a fire. I placed my hands on the door handles, wondering how hot they would need to be before my skin burnt and blistered. I timed how long it took to jump out of bed and run from our bedroom, through the lounge room, past the dining room, down the passageway, and to the kids' rooms. Eight seconds. After I pictured myself dragging a drowned toddler out of our pool, I went out seven or eight times a day to make sure the pool gate was securely latched. Even on rainy nights, I ran out in the dark, jiggling it back and forth to be sure. Such was my nightly ritual that whenever I chastised the kids for not locking up before they went to bed, they replied there was no need because they knew I'd be up through the night doing my security rounds.

As my obsessions grew, I was haunted by the news of a baby who'd died after being left in a hot car and compulsively turned around to check the back seat when I drove to work on stiflingly hot summer days. What if a phantom child found their way in and I unknowingly locked them in, leaving them to suffocate in the heat? I imagined Michael being set upon, becoming the latest victim of the spate of one-punch coward attacks that had recently claimed the lives of boys not much older than him—boys whose only crime was a night out with their friends. Whenever James worked away, which was several nights a week, I invented headlines of his car being T-boned by a tattooed, ice-addicted, bikie gang leader in a wild police chase through the streets of Sydney. My mind showed me the mangled wreck that might take my husband away.

These images were irrational and sickening, without perspective or boundaries, so I dreaded where they might take me next. I tried to push them away, but they developed into little paranoias, and I operated on high alert because danger lurked in every corner of my mind. As my state of mind deteriorated, I wondered, *How did a blessed life become so tormented?*

CHAPTER 5
SOMETHING'S UP

Early on a warm December morning two months after the episode, I strap Atlantis, my trusty SUP, to the roof racks just as the first streaks of scarlet flush the sky. I'm resigned now to pre-dawn restlessness and head to the beach, taking advantage of having the roads to myself, except for the tradies who are also dawn risers and fit in a quick surf on their way to building sites. Soon the *tat-tat-tat* of hydraulic power will add to the pulse of coast life as councils try to keep up with the steady influx of tourists already making their way here for the Christmas season.

However, the city is still waking up, and the morning stretches sleepily; drowsy baristas prepare for the morning onslaught. As the sun rises, it shines millions of tiny mirrors over the water, which play together like children who chase each other through the surf. The reflection catches my eye, and I'm blinded for a split second by the glare.

It reminds me of bored kids at school assemblies who re-enact this mischief of nature by angling their watches into the sun, creating a dancing speck of light over a wall or on the back of one of their peers, using it as a canvas for their own light show. The bolder ones aim directly at someone's face, torchlike, and their hapless victim is forced to squint and look away. It makes me smile because it reminds me that times haven't changed all that much.

****

What else can we measure ourselves by than what we used to do and now can't? In the months following my panic attack, my measure of normal was anything I was able to do previously. James had bought me a stand-up paddleboard for Christmas one summer, and I christened her after the brand name—Atlantis—an alluring, watery evocation of the lost city. Her fins sliced the water as I harnessed the breezes of the beach, which can feel deceptively gentler onshore. On weekends, I sometimes paddled for hours.

In a family where I was the only one who didn't play just about any sport on offer, this was one I could claim. Sometimes I used it as a mini wharf and jumped off for a swim. Sometimes it became a giant kickboard. On lazy afternoons, I floated on it and went wherever the wind blew me.

Most often, I enjoyed standing up and paddling, exploring the ocean, venturing over small reefs where a sea turtle occasionally popped its head up, peering around curiously before disappearing below the surface. Stingrays, partly camouflaged by the sand, appeared to levitate along the seabed, playing hide-and-seek with the shadow of the board. I dangled my legs in the water and watched sea birds dive and then ride the wind. Jumping fish took flight as they darted up and out of the ocean. I loved the sense of freedom the board gave me, and I paddled out to the boats anchored offshore, drifting luxuriously between them, listening to the water lapping against their hulls. I'd tried surfing on it where small waves roll in at the mouth of the Maroochy River, and in pre-episode days, falling off was part of the fun.

Now, I wearily unloaded the board and dragged it down to the sand, where it lay, neglected and ignored, while I hid behind a book. I stared at the pages and tried to still the game of ping pong that played out in my head.

What are you waiting for?

I'll go in later.

Why don't you go in now?

I don't know. Shut up. I'm trying to read.

Look! Those people are on their boards, so why don't you get on yours?

I will. Do you think the swell is too big?

Are you serious? There is no swell!

What if I fall in?

You've fallen in heaps of times. There's no point bringing the board if you're not going to use it.

Fine.

I watched as early morning swimmers lapped between the Spit and the main beach of Mooloolaba. These were not the young, muscled bodies of the surf lifesaving squads undertaking mock rescues, nor were they the sleek pre-teen nippers who trained each weekend by running flag relays in the sand and paddling out to ride the rips of the ocean. These swimmers were older than me, men and women defiant in their refusal to let age deny them their ocean workout. Many mornings I watched as their graceful strokes, slow but strong, carried them remarkable distances across the water and back again. Today their stamina only made me doubt my own.

Tentatively, I put the board in the water and sat on it, pretending to enjoy the moment with the boaties who baited their hooks and cast the first lines of the day. In the distance, children scurried along the rock wall and out to the beacon. They peered curiously into the buckets of fishermen, attached like human barnacles to rocks strewn with wet seaweed dumped by an outgoing tide. Kayakers cut the water with enviable synergy. The breeze blew white foam onto the sand, teasing an overweight bitzer whose frenzied barks were proof that I was the only one stalling. I turned my attention back to the board, knowing I was playing for time because I was too scared to stand up.

When I eventually did, instead of looking straight ahead into the horizon to centre my weight, instead of riding the ocean and using its energy to glide across the surface, my body fought against it so that I jerked stiffly and overbalanced. I climbed back up and looked down into the depths of the water beneath me, hoping to God I didn't see anything, like a shark. The *Jaws* theme song played in my head, competing with Newton's law; I tested his theory that for every action there is an equal and opposite reaction, and as my grip on reality unravelled, my grip on the paddle tightened, turning it into a weapon.

Conjuring the heart-stopping images of Mick Fanning's encounter with the great white in South Africa, I was as unstable in my mind as I was in my legs. Every little ripple threatened to send me toppling. I looked over to Mooloolaba and wanted to paddle there on my board like the other paddlers, like I'd done many times before, but I sat back down, defeated, and skulked back onto the shore, feeling pathetic.

Being afraid of something I'd previously found exhilarating, something I'd done so many times before, wasn't normal. Back-and-forth conversations with myself, where I actually heard my own voices, were also not normal. Nor was having no memory of whole conversations that had taken place. Everybody has moments of forgetfulness, but I recognised a red flag when these happened several times a day. Sitting on the beach hiding behind a book and leaving the paddleboard dumped on the sand all day was not my normal.

And yet, I was acutely aware of the energy surrounding me. The day was literally awash with life, as though the world was showing me the joy that waited on the other side of illness. If you watch closely enough, the tempo of beach life becomes distinctive; people come and go like the tide—families, lovers, idle beach walkers, boys and girls who rough and tumble through the space between childhood and the more serious pursuit of growing up. And so it was that day: young mums built sandcastles with their toddlers; families threw lunchtime leftovers to seagulls who squawked and squabbled like their children fraying in the sun; teenage boys showed off for their girlfriends, swimming out as far as they dared toward the horizon; and a young couple submersed shoulder deep, became paper silhouettes against the dimming skyline.

The day gradually cooled, beckoning older folk who wandered hand in hand along the water's edge. *What hardships have they endured?* I wondered. *What secrets have they kept?* The softening embers of dusk descended, and the last of the summer day danced briefly with the sea. As I watched, I knew I had to find a way to catch the light again and hold on to it. I just didn't know how.

CHAPTER 6
BECOMING UNSTUCK

Seeking solace, we spent a quiet Christmas in Tasmania that year. The extended holiday break meant I could focus on getting myself 'right'. We walked around Dove Lake, cradled by the mountain landscapes that frame it. I read self-help tips on social media as well as articles about panic attacks and anxiety.

I dislodged unwelcome thoughts by flicking through travel magazines and drank warm herbal tea, seeking comfort in peppermint, liquorice, and ginger. I tried to read books—a holiday luxury—but couldn't focus enough to persevere, and they lay aborted and abandoned after only a few chapters.

Back home, while I couldn't conquer my bizarre fear of paddleboarding, I went to the beach and waded in the shallows. I approached life slowly and with caution, much like the guardians of the Maroochy River—the pelicans—who drifted gently with the current at dusk. I'm sure the restorative effect of nature was connected to a rhythm that meandered rather than rushed. The initial panic I'd felt immediately following the attack wasn't so raw, but as we welcomed in 2017, and with it the commencement of a new, frenetic school year, I felt the flutter of nausea beckoning.

I stepped away from my position as year-level coordinator and returned to classroom teaching. To achieve a better work-life balance, I also reduced my teaching load to a part-time basis. Suspecting I was experiencing something more than a one-off panic attack, I'd done some reading and discovered that I ticked some of the boxes for anxiety and some for burnout. But these were little more than semi-educated guesses, and simply suspecting something of a more serious nature left room for being wrong—a definite diagnosis would make it real.

I avoided explaining to family and friends that I wasn't coping and was unwilling to accept that my symptoms wouldn't pass, given enough time. Aside from nausea, the pain I felt wasn't physical, which made it easier to deny. Although I hadn't returned to the doctor since my visit in October, I had explored the myriad mental health apps available online and found them helpful; bite-sized chunks of information and simple infographics were easy to digest. I even subscribed to an online newsletter but got cold feet and cancelled the subscription when I received a personalised message on my phone.

As expected, the first week back at school was an explosion of life. Classrooms that had been dormant over the holiday period now pulsed with energy. Shrieks of delight filled the air as students reunited with their friends. Laughter was interspersed with tears as juniors—big kids now in high school—tried to decipher their timetables.

School was a high-octane melting pot of activity as kids jostled and chased each other through the yard, wrestled with stubborn lockers, and argued over the rules of handball. Lunchtime meetings were held to organise clubs and carnivals. And to top it all off, I was a group leader on a three-day welcome-to-high-school camp for 173 students who didn't know each other very well.

Carnivals and camps are the glue of school spirit, but the thought of facing the demands of these high-energy, often unpredictable days sent me further into a spiral of self-doubt. Here was another red flag, more evidence that my 'normal' world had changed, a slap-in-the-face reminder of what I used to be able to do but now couldn't—and knowing this brought me even more unstuck. This internal discord made the thought of the fast-approaching three-day camp an almost impossible feat.

These days, camps don't get off the ground without the all-important risk assessment—a document that rivals the current legal studies textbook for detail. Teachers are on duty 24/7 and inevitably stay up tending to students who get homesick or sugar-sick, or both. Thirty years ago, kids mostly stayed in bed, but these days the goal seems to be spending as much time as possible out of bed, pulling off dorm raids and sneaking into whichever out-of-bounds areas are left unguarded. By the third day, tempers simmer and threaten to boil over as tolerance levels decline for sleep-deprived staff and students alike.

Managing the number of children who suffer from allergies, anxiety, depression, eating disorders, impulsive behaviours, oppositional defiance, attention deficit disorders, and other conditions is something I don't recall being quite as much of an issue for me when I first started teaching.

If they stay in the game long enough, teachers develop a razor-sharp radar for danger. I did. However, a painstakingly completed risk assessment, irrespective of how detailed, doesn't prevent accidents and injury to students. Regardless of how carefully I supervised and how vigilant I was, things could go terribly wrong.

I'd learned this first-hand the night a school disco turned from the macarena into a game of stacks-on in a split second. When a group of over-excited boys ran into the centre of the room and piled on top of each other, one was pinned at the bottom of the heap and couldn't move or make himself heard above the music. Despite the teachers rushing over to untangle the splayed legs and arms that formed a human centrepiece on the dancefloor, he spent the night in hospital with a concussion.

I'd learned it again when thirteen-year-old Sarah, a year eight student, fell from high ropes equipment during a recreation camp near

Ewen Maddock Dam and was stretchered into an ambulance with a broken back. Although I hadn't been on that camp, back at school, we all held our breath while we waited for news of her prognosis.

I was just as worried for the other students who were in Sarah's camp group and for my devastated colleagues who'd witnessed the accident. Despite not being to blame, you always feel responsible when children get hurt. We all felt the weight of the headlines that screamed: 'Classmate Horror as Girl Falls'.[3]

Sarah, a passionate dancer, lay in a hospital bed awaiting the results of tests to see if she would walk again.[4] Thankfully, with the assistance of a back brace, Sarah gradually recovered. When I ran into her parents at a school function not long afterwards, I was reminded that nothing is more important than being entrusted with other people's children.

In a somewhat less dire incident, a student was whisked off for a tetanus shot after being bitten by a donkey. While central and northern Australia is home to millions of feral donkeys brought to the country in the 1800s as pack animals, dangerous donkeys are not something we'd normally anticipate on the Sunshine Coast. So, when the teacher in charge came back to school, she made us all laugh as she threw her arms up in the staffroom and demanded of the heavens, 'What was I bloody well thinking when I left donkey bite off the risk assessment?!'

These experiences, and others like them, had taught me to be diligent and alert. But as we departed for camp, my duty-of-care barometer surged, and I felt out of place among the high spirits of everyone else. I was so preoccupied with the students' safety that they could hardly blink without me running a mental safety audit.

I watched the non-swimmers like a hawk, checked on the children who had anaphylactic reactions to wasps and bee stings, and those whose medical forms listed allergies to march flies and green ant bites. All biting insects became the enemy, and I eyed nesting magpies with suspicion.

I made sure the specially prepared lactose-free, egg-free, nut-free, and gluten-free meals passed quality control and asked to see the sugar-level readings of the diabetics. I carried out regular inventories of the EpiPens and asthma puffers the students were supposed to always carry on them but inevitably got left behind as they moved from one activity to the next. I'd even bought a watch with a second hand in case I needed to time the duration of a seizure.

Had I remembered to distribute everyone's medication? This student had anxiety. That one's impulsivity would get him hurt, or, sure enough, the innocent who happened to be standing next to him. I kept a close eye on them both and made a mental note to make sure Mister Impulsive was my canoeing partner.

Were they all harnessed in properly? What if someone fell, or wandered off, or got burnt by the fire? What if the snacks we'd forbidden, but knew would be smuggled in for late-night dorm parties, contained life-threatening allergens? What if, what if, what if …? All these questions crowded my thinking and further imposed upon my state of mind.

I watched kids zipline through uncertainty on flying foxes and take the dreaded leap of faith, balancing precariously on top of a pole, which, just like the beanstalk, was so high that it disappeared into the clouds—then leap off into the metaphorical unknown.

They built rafts to keep themselves afloat, not just in the artificial lake but in the River of Life. They climbed giant ladders that forced them to look up and aim high. On the second night, the Wandering Wombats came in well after dark, tired and hungry, waiting for as long as it took for everyone in their group to conquer the challenge and return to camp feeling like heroes.

By contrast, I was feeling anything but heroic, ducking and dodging my way around high-energy days, shrinking from anything that meant taking risks. Mostly, I felt like a fraud. Here I was shouting placards like: 'You can do it', 'Jump on three', 'You are stronger than you think'. I watched these kids face their fears head-on, their little voices and skinny legs shaking with fear but jumping anyway.

Meanwhile, I couldn't even stand up on my own paddleboard. Not leading by example elevated my feelings of failure. As I shied away from the very experiences that had provided me with a sense of purpose and connection, I felt dispirited and hollow. An emptiness grew. It picked away slowly at the glue that had, up until this point, bound me to school life, and it would become harder and harder to hold on.

CHAPTER 7

LOSS

Despite feeling anxious about the commencement of the school year post-episode, I hoped that if I could wait it out, my symptoms would dissipate. I had managed to survive camp—just—and was ready to meet my new classes. The Year 7 students had come from primary school with the reputation of being 'a lovely group', but a question from a student in the second week back would set the tone for a tough year. There was no malice in her question, but it sliced the room. 'What's with the pictures of that kid who was murdered?' she asked, too flippantly.

Lucy* was a Year 7 girl with a what-you-see-is-what-you-get personality. She felt but didn't understand the stony silence that answered her back. But I did. A vertical homeroom structure consisting of all year levels meant the older students had an advantage over newbies like Lucy, who didn't yet know the important stories. Many senior students come to see themselves as the stewards of tradition, the 'keepers of the customs', which shape the ethos referred to in school mission statements. It is right that schools should talk explicitly of ethos, of integrity and character, but it is always human emotion, not tradition, that evokes the most powerful responses from students. Lucy's question drew a tangible resentment from the others in the class, which, as a new girl, she could not be expected to understand.

'Come on, Luce,' I said just as the bell went. 'We're going for a walk. I want to show you something.'

I invited her outside and took her to Daniel's chair, a memorial to Daniel Morcombe established by his cohort when they graduated. In his memory, they installed a wooden seat—a waiting chair—as a promise they would wait for him. This was a special place—a peaceful place I'd used as a talking seat with other students, too. We sat down together, and I asked Lucy to read the simple inscription on the plaque mounted to the timber frame. She read it out loud:

> *Daniel's Chair*
> *For our Friend*
> *Daniel Morcombe*
> *Seniors of 2006*

'Do you know who Daniel was?' I asked.

'Yes, he's the boy who went missing,' she said. She scuffed the side of her shoe along the cement, trying to work out what this had to do with her. Daniel didn't go missing; he was taken, but that's a conversation for adults, so I said, 'He did. He was also a student here, and we miss him every day. The boy in the picture is Daniel.' I paused, giving her time to put it all together.

As we sat, I told her Daniel's story and the impact of this on our school. I explained that Daniel's mum and dad, and sometimes his brother, came to the yearly awards night to present a special trophy in his honour. That every year, we joined the Walk for Daniel to remember him and to support the work the Morcombe Foundation does to keep kids safe. But most importantly, I let her know that like the inscription says, Daniel was and remains our friend.

Lucy nodded, understanding things better, and stopped destroying her shoe. Then she asked, 'How old was he?'

Daniel spent his last day of school in 2003 at the traditional end-of-year beach barbecue, during which he spoke to a teacher about his upcoming fourteenth birthday party that he was sharing with his twin brother, Bradley. Daniel complained that his parents had made a 'no girls' rule, and the girls listening to the story commiserated—as Daniel's friends, they would have loved to go to the party. Daniel died four days later, waiting for a bus to take him to Sunshine Plaza to buy Christmas presents for his family. Years later, the teacher told Daniel's parents this story, and Bruce replied that they'd never made the 'no girls' rule. He guessed Daniel said it to not hurt their feelings.

I didn't teach Daniel, but I lived his story the same way the rest of the nation did. I often had to drive past the site of his abduction but couldn't bring myself to look at it. People continued to leave flowers beneath the Kiel Mountain Road overpass, but my gut wrenched each time I drove past, and I turned my head away.

When Daniel's funeral occurred on 7 December 2012, I was asked to distribute communion during the requiem mass. It was a time of deep sadness for us all. While we were finally able to say goodbye and lay him to rest, the sorrow and pain of losing him came flooding back. The service was held in St Catherine's Church, which is situated on campus. The school liaised with Daniel's family, the media, and with security. As mourners gathered, our school grounds became a symbolic sea of red, the colour of the T-shirt Daniel was last seen wearing while he waited for the bus. The scene was punctuated by funeral-black attire and the high-visibility vests of SES volunteers, some of whom had been involved in the search. Among those in attendance were former Prime Minister Kevin Rudd, former Queensland Police Commissioner Bob Atkinson, and then Queensland Police Commissioner Ian Stewart.

A projector screen was erected on the grounds outside the church for the large numbers who came to pay their respects. Media cameras moved discreetly among them while journalists gave their broadcasts. It was a strange, sombre transformation of our school, where only the day before I'd reminded a group of students to tuck their shirts in. How petty that seemed now. How very insignificant. Today, every shirt was tucked, every belt buckled, every tie straight. Ponytails were neatly tied with red ribbon. Socks were pulled up, and shoes were polished. For Daniel.

Although I've never met Bruce and Denise, I felt, as many did, that I knew them. It was important for me to make sure the minor part for which I was responsible went smoothly. It would be the only thing I would ever be able to do for them, and I wanted to do it with as much grace as they have. I didn't allow my children, who were in primary school—Michael in year five, Cate in year two—to attend the funeral because I didn't want to be distracted by the need to comfort them.

As the crowd gathered, I was struck by the number of young people who packed into the church and spilled out onto the grounds. As they came forward to receive communion, I knew many of them were former classmates who had returned to say goodbye. They had waited and grieved, and I wanted them to feel welcome in this school, which would always be theirs. Their presence contributed to the healing that, after too many years, might finally begin. In his eulogy, Bruce told them not to be sad and asked them instead to embrace Daniel's return to his family. I wanted them to know that even after they'd left school, we continued to sit on the waiting chair to wait for their friend. I felt the power of being in communion with those who gathered at the school, those who attended from their lounge rooms, those who grieved across the country, and I felt Daniel's presence too.

When the funeral ended, we made our way from the church to the Daintree—the name of the school hall. There were mountains of food piled on trestle tables that stretched across the room, untouched.

People milled about, talking quietly in groups, making room for each other as they reconnected with past friends and teachers.

Normally, we'd be making our way to the Alexandra Surf Club for our staff Christmas lunch on the last day of school, but we knew nobody would feel like celebrating. Instead, we'd directed the Christmas funds to the spread of food that people gradually started to pick at. Glad to have something to do, I offered around a plate of sandwiches. It's strange what you remember; as I moved among the crowd, I thought, *I'm going to let the kids have white-bread sandwiches in their lunches next year.* I don't know why I thought that—my thoughts were turning up uninvited.

Many of the faces I knew—students, colleagues, parents—and many I didn't because they were a part of the story before my time. I recognised Hetty Johnston, lobbyist and founder of Bravehearts, an organisation that advocates for better child protection in Australia. I wanted to thank her for keeping the important issue of child protection in the spotlight. If I'd been able to speak, I would have told her how grateful I was for her work in making sure the welfare of our children is at the centre of policy and decision making. I would have told her nothing is more important than making the world a safer place for our kids. I would have urged her to never stop shining a spotlight on how our system sometimes fails them and the tragic statistics of those who die at the hands of child sex offenders.

If I'd been able to speak, I would have said all this, but my words got stuck in my grief and remained unsaid. In the days that followed, I cried. A lot. The heartache, the sadness of the world without Daniel, became grief for all children we had failed to protect. As a mother and a teacher, there is no deeper pain. When the days became weeks and the tears wouldn't stop, I flew to Adelaide to seek refuge with my friend Helen.

I first met Helen in Mount Gambier, South Australia, midway through 1990, when we were both young teachers starting out in regional schools in the southeast wine region. Her name means 'shining light', and in the weeks following Daniel's funeral, I needed some of it to lift the darkness, which seemed to have settled over my heart and wouldn't shift. Helen met me at the airport, hugged me and let me cry. She took me to lunch at one of our old haunts at Port Noarlunga, and as she is always in charge of ordering the wine, she did so matter-of-factly, one of those well-entrenched hallmarks of a friendship that picks up where it left off.

She listened as I blubbered my way through lunch. There wasn't much to listen to besides a word or two gulped out between sobs, drowned by wine I couldn't taste. Every now and then, she questioned me gently, allowing me to recognise and understand my grief. And then she just sat in it with me until my sadness gradually became less lonely, but no less heavy. My grief for Daniel became a lingering melancholy that followed me home.

Even then, four years before the panic attack, I was aware of a growing heaviness that made it harder to recover from life's heartbreaks. There was no doubt I felt the depths of my sadness pulling at me for weeks, months, even years before it grew too big for me to carry. However, at the time of Daniel's funeral, I didn't recognise the warning signs because my tears were camouflaged among the tears of everyone at school. We were all sad, and my tears were no wetter than anyone else's.

In the months following the funeral, when people had recovered enough from their initial grief to start talking about Daniel in normal conversation, I fell silent and still couldn't speak through my sadness. Perhaps I should have asked myself some honest questions then, but I told myself that everyone deals with grief differently, and I pushed it away. I simply didn't pay enough attention to the cracks.

Strangely, even as a kid, I named grief as my number one fear. Deep into the night when sleepovers with girlfriends looked like midnight feasts, games of truth and dare, and snuggled up in pyjamas, our girl-talk morphed into questions like, 'What are you most afraid of?' something inside me whispered: *Grief*. I'd felt its cruelty when my childhood friend, a beautiful soul who was braver than any nine-year-old girl should ever have to be, lost her battle with brain cancer. Our birthdays were just ten days apart. I thought of my friend at the oddest times. When I got my first bikini. When I kissed Lee Hunter behind the hall after youth group. And although she would have been way too gentle for punk rock, I thought of her when I was fifteen, on my first real date, watching Adam and the Ants live at the Apollo Stadium in Adelaide. She would have hated it.

Lottie* and I spent Saturday mornings stretched out like starfish on her bedroom floor, colouring in and cutting out paper clothes to dress our paper dolls. I cried when her soft brown hair fell out in chunks and when she became so pale I could see the fine blue veins, as delicate as lace, through her skin. I cried when the tumour grew bigger and she couldn't colour in anymore because she started to lose her vision and couldn't see the lines. And when she died, I cried because I was young, too, and didn't know how to be a better friend. I couldn't bear to see her parents stumble through grief so painful it nearly killed them too, knowing that despite never giving up, they couldn't save their little girl. So, I'd seen the way grief made people crumple and how the crushing sadness never really goes away.

I felt sadness like this again in 1991, during my initial teaching post in South Australia. A call from the principal came over the PA system, asking all teachers on campus to gather in the staff room. We knew an impromptu staff meeting wasn't good, but when he told us one of our junior boys had taken his own life and had been found that morning, we were devastated. Inexperienced and unprepared for a blow like this, the tragic and unexpected loss of a young life blindsided me.

We were hurriedly briefed and then went outside to support students as they arrived. These were the days before mobile phones, but in regional communities, the bush telegraph moved just as fast. As I consoled groups of students who'd gathered and were already mourning their friend, I had the sensation of fractured time and muffled sound. I would have this same feeling many years later, in the weeks following the episode in 2016.

One of the parents I'd befriended was a social worker who came to the school to help counsel the students. When she saw me, she explained that I could be in a state of shock. This would account for the out-of-body sensation I encountered as I roamed the schoolyard, feeling disconnected from everything that was unfolding around me. I tried hard to be professional by pushing aside my emotional response. I tried to comfort distraught students who cried together in sad little friendship huddles. But as a new teacher, I was out of my depth.

All funerals are sad, but the pain is almost unbearable when we bury our children. Standing amid the inconsolable heartache of a young boy's funeral, holding the Order of Service numbly in my hand, I felt the impossibility of letting him go. I felt the loss of words not yet spoken, of lessons not yet learned, of kindnesses not yet shown, of loves not yet kindled. His death ripped a hole in the natural order of things, and even today, if I'm called to an unplanned staff meeting, I struggle to quell the nausea rising in my stomach, hoping I won't have to attend another student's funeral. Hoping that I'll never again hear the guttural cry of a boy's father as he calls out for his son, his grief crumpling us all. I'd never heard pain like the choking call for a lost child, and I've never forgotten what a broken man sounds like.

Sadly, since then, I have attended the funerals of too many students. And the world dims each time I do. Road fatalities, sporting tragedies, cruel illnesses, suicides. The passing of time is constantly visible in schools, punctuated by bells and measured in weeks, terms, semesters. It's marked at graduation dinners, speech nights, formals, and guards of honour as students, parents, and teachers proudly celebrate important milestones. On these occasions, an empty chair, a missing voice, a college jersey not worn is an aching reminder of the ones who should be there but aren't. I never stop missing those children. I never stop feeling the loss of them—not even for a day. And there's a shard of anger within the sadness, a seething grief that bleeds into the sky. Not because I think that's where spirit resides, but because sometimes skies heave too with grey-laden sorrow, because the sky hears me whisper, 'But we hadn't finished.'

****

While I was in Adelaide seeking Helen's counsel after Daniel's funeral, one of her friends, Anne, gave me a journal. No doubt there's a psychological reason why I think better with a pen in my hand and why I don't feel the same satisfaction when I read a book I can't hold, just as there's probably a psychological reason why I can't work in a cluttered room. My thoughts were in disarray, and words evaded me then, but the journal became an important tool, nonetheless.

It became a scrapbook of flotsam and jetsam—a collection of quotes, pictures, disjointed ideas, and the scribblings of disconnected thoughts. Interestingly, the word flotsam derives from an Old French word, *floteson*, meaning to float, and jetsam, a contracted form of 'jettison', which refers to debris thrown overboard by the crew of a ship in distress to lighten the ship's load. It's an apt description of Anne's gift, which helped me to stay afloat not just then, but in the times of grief and emotional chaos that followed.

It was a long time before I could talk about Daniel or read about him in the press without crying. Even now, it's touch and go. The photograph most often used by the media shows a beautiful boy whose eyes shine with hope for a future that will never come. The makeshift memorial beneath the Kiel Mountain Road overpass has become a permanent monument flanked by olive trees symbolising peace. But I still can't bring myself to look at it and avoid driving past it.

****

The thing about grief, and perhaps the reason I wanted to run from it, is that it keeps coming back. It grabs you when you hear a laugh in the distance, or catch a smell, or read a headline. It grabs you in the line of a song, or a look, or a circumstance that might ordinarily be of no consequence. A circumstance as ordinary as two boys being late for class in term three, 2017. Post-episode and in an already fragile state of mind, my thoughts took me to extremes, and I fought to keep a lid on the rising anxiety that threatened to spill over on a day when two junior boys were a no-show to my class. They were there at lunchtime—I'd seen them playing touch football on the oval. We called them over the PA system but got no response. I rang student services to ask if they'd signed out early, but according to our records, they were still at school. Except they weren't. I checked in with their friends, but no-one had seen them since the touch footy game.

Unsettling questions poked me, making it impossible to focus on anything else. Were they hiding somewhere to skip afternoon classes? Had they nicked out through the back gate to the shops? The slurpies there were popular. I tried to stay calm by focusing on the students in the class but kept glancing through the window of my classroom for signs that we'd located them. *What if somebody else finds them before we do?* I thought.

'Can I go to the library please, Miss? My book's overdue,' asked one of the girls, but I fobbed her off.

'Not now,' I said. 'Maybe tomorrow.'

'Can I go to the bubblers and fill up my water bottle?' asked another.

'Miss, I've lost my hat—can I go and check in the lost property?

'Miss, I need to go and print out—' I cut them off and raised my voice loudly enough for the whole class to hear, 'No! Nobody's going anywhere. Sit in your seats so I can see everyone is where they're supposed to be!' My tone was terse, and they weren't used to me snapping at them.

Now subdued, they sat quietly, and I was struck by how innocent they still were. I pushed away images of Tiahleigh Palmer, a young girl the same age whose body was found on the bank of the Pimpama River just outside of Brisbane in 2015.[5] I tried not to think about Daniel. *Your mind's running away with you now;* I heard James's voice alerting me that my fear was taking over, something he'd started doing when he noticed the warning signs. *Kids skip classes all the time*, I told myself. *It's almost a rite of passage in high school.* But I felt myself drifting, and I kept looking at the intercom on the wall, willing it to ring.

Thankfully, it did just before the end of the lesson, and the boys turned up safe and sound. In trouble, but safe. Alive.

On days such as this, my fear left a sick aftertaste, and I imagined what *could* have happened. Even when students produced signed permission notes from their parents to dismiss them directly from an excursion venue, I rang to make sure they'd made it home safely.

'Oh, hi,' said one parent when I called them after a school swimming carnival. 'How lovely of you to ring and check. Yes, everyone's home—all good. They had a great day at the carnival, by the way. They'll sleep well tonight!'

Little did she know I was ringing because if I didn't, I'd be swallowing the acrid-tasting backwash of my imagination all weekend.

Michael started high school in 2015, three years after Daniel's funeral, and he was frustrated by my ultra-cautious reluctance to let him go anywhere on his own. Chafing at the bit for more independence, he mistook this for not trusting him and pleaded with me in exasperation.

'Mum, you can trust me. What do you think is going to happen?'

'It's not that I don't trust you, Mike,' I said. 'It's that I don't always trust other people. I'll let you do things on your own, I promise. I know *you're* ready. It's that *I'm* not ready yet.'

'When *will* you be ready?' he asked, feeling the bite of not being allowed to ride his bike or skate to the shops like many of his friends were allowed to do.

'I'm not sure. I'll let you know.'

Despite not feeling completely ready, I gradually released him to greater levels of independence, and it seemed like I barely had enough time to get used to it before Cate had reached her first year of high school and was keen to explore the world without me. Unfortunately for her, my readiness regressed when she became a casualty of stranger danger.

I'd reluctantly agreed to let her go to the local shops by herself for the first time, but only if she took her phone and our dog, Max. Just five minutes after she left the house, she sent an SMS asking me to come and get her. I rang her phone, and my skin prickled at the sound of her voice. I jumped into the car and raced to where she was waiting, Max sitting obediently beside her.

When she saw me, she burst into tears; a man had followed her and offered her lollies, which he had in his pocket. He'd questioned her about where she lived and where her parents were. Thankfully, she knew to get herself to the shopping centre where there was high visibility and wait for me there. She described him as middle-aged, neatly groomed with a red hat. I drove around in the hope that we might be able to spot him, but he'd seemingly vanished into thin air.

When she asked me from the back seat of the car what we would do if we saw him, I replied, too calmly for my liking, that we would run him over and break his legs and then call the police. I glanced in the rear-vision mirror, wishing labradors looked more vicious. I'm thankful we never found that man—an evil cliché in a red hat—because I'm not sure what I might have been capable of.

Not too long after that incident, I took my English class into the library to borrow our class novel. I opened mine, and it had Daniel's name in it; he'd borrowed the book before me. I touched the pages lightly, glad that his name continued to be spoken in our school. Daniel was our friend, and we waited for him.

CHAPTER 8
OUTSIDE THE STADIUM

September promised the pinnacle of school events—Carnival Day! Every year, the quadrangle became a high school amusement park filled with kids—unrecognisable at first—in T-shirts and shorts instead of school uniforms. The doughnut stall competed with the ice cream stand—an impossible choice for those who'd spend most of their money in the first hour. With 900 sugar-high teenagers, Carnival Day was the embodiment of the adage 'It's all fun and games until somebody gets hurt', and sure enough, every year I crawled headfirst into the jumping castle to rescue the ones who got pummelled.

Teachers volunteered for the dunking machine—the most popular revenge-seeking attraction of the day. In this event, students aimed at their teacher, who sat, prone, on a wet seat that snapped open and dropped us without warning. We'd climb back up again, shivering, and taunt them into buying another three shots for a dollar.

'Come on,' we'd yell into the crowd gathered to watch the show. 'Take your best sho—' And then someone would hit the bullseye, plunging their teacher into ice-cold water. Delighted cheers followed as we resurfaced, our clothes fully soaked, and the score for assigning too much homework was settled in the most satisfying of ways.

Not that year, though. As Carnival Day, 2017 approached, I realised with a sinking feeling that I couldn't risk being dunked. It already felt too much like I was drowning.

I previously looked forward to carnivals because of their energy and unpredictability, because they brought a welcome change of routine and opportunities for kids to be themselves. Such was the case at the carnival the year before when, on impulse, a student performed a stand-up comedy routine in front of the entire school.

I crossed my fingers as she walked out and hoped she had a well-rehearsed skit, knowing that even with the help of a microphone, we would not be able to keep a 900-strong teenage audience in line if it went bad.

As she warmed up, she unearthed a hidden talent, mimicking one teacher after another in a hilarious parody that brought the whole assembly, teachers included, to their feet. When the place erupted into a spontaneous, heartfelt standing ovation, our young comedienne threw her arms up and revelled in the applause as her peers clapped and *whoop-whooped* madly.

I remember looking out into the cheering crowd of young people and seeing the importance of providing kids with reasons to buy in—to be lifted by the power of each other's potential. I am yet to meet a child who isn't drawn into joy; the soul almost won't allow it.

These are moments when life overflows and 'nobody gets left behind'—words that became the theme for a junior camp one year. Having known the intoxication of life overflowing, I felt the emptiness I now carried even more deeply. The deafening cheers of students brimming with life was a grating contrast to the long silences I disappeared into. Having once felt the synergy of working alongside my colleagues, I now felt estranged from them.

Teaching is so much about intuition, and now that I no longer trusted mine, I was nervous about stepping into unpredictable environments. So, I opted out by ringing in sick. And each time I did—for Carnival Day and several times a term—my moral compass felt misaligned. I felt as though I was somehow betraying what I believed in—that the earth's axis had tilted and I wasn't standing where I should be.

I felt like a coward and a liar each time I rang in sick because I hadn't yet accepted that I was. Disconnected, yes. Exhausted, yes. Fearful and forgetful, yes. Anxious and panicked at times? Yes. But not really, truly sick.

I hoped my avoidance would not be seen as disinterest because this was not the case. In fact, I lived quite close to my school, so after I called in sick on Carnival Day, I sat outside on the back deck, listening to the sounds of school spirit as they drifted across the oval. While I shied away from taking part in the celebrations, I didn't like feeling what the kids call FOMO (fear of missing out). I tracked the events in my mind and tried to convince myself that I was still connected. *I'm there in spirit*, I told myself.

Sitting on the deck that day, I was reminded of a Year 8 activity where students draw a sports stadium. They draw the field, adding score lines, goal posts, and benches. Some put in VIP sections. Others include floodlights and scoreboards. When they've completed their design, we ask them to draw themselves in the picture. Are they centre field where all the action is or right at the back in the docks watching the game from a distance? Are they sidelined or on the bench because of a penalty? They consider how comfortable they are there and whether they'd like to draw themselves somewhere else. Of course, this activity is designed to challenge students about where they are in the game of life and where they want to be.

I realised that not only was I off the field, but I wasn't even in the stadium. And for a long time, I just couldn't get my head back in the game. Most mornings before my panic attack, I'd call out a casual tongue-in-cheek goodbye to James as I headed off to school, saying, 'I'm off to shape the young minds of the future.' Now, the goalposts had shifted. I didn't have the energy or the desire to change the world anymore; I just wanted to find a way to be a part of it.

CHAPTER 9
MEDUSA

One of the benefits of working part time was that some mornings were later starts. After an early morning walk, I still had time to call in to the supermarket before school to stock up on supplies: sticky notes, click-top pens, and a packet of chocolate frogs I kept on hand for quiz prizes and bribes. One morning, an elderly driver struggled to swing his car out of a narrow car park, so I stopped to give him room. Perhaps I stopped too quickly because a glance in my rear-view mirror showed a wild-haired woman gesturing furiously in the car behind. She huffed out of her vehicle and headed straight for me, hair and temper flaring.

In my mind's eye, I pictured Medusa ready to strike anyone who wasn't quick enough to get out of the way: in this case, me. Instinctively, I locked the car door, which was just as well because she marched over to my window, her face centimetres from mine, and blasted my mellow morning into oblivion.

'Wind down the fuckin' window!' Spit droplets spattered the glass.

No fuckin' fear, I thought. This felt strange because it sounds weird when teachers swear, even in their heads. I sank further into the driver's seat, not only to hide from her but also from the council workers who'd stopped their tree trimming to watch the fracas. I froze with fear and burned with humiliation at the same time.

Scenes of road rage, black eyes, and bruised faces on the six o'clock news flashed before me, and there was no way I was getting

63

out of the car. I pictured my own grab: *Students gathered to pay their respects to an unsuspecting teacher who was stabbed this morning in a supermarket car park. The murder weapon, a retractable pen, was found by council workers who witnessed the attack.*

I remembered the myth—anyone who looked at Medusa turned to stone—and hastily averted my eyes. This infuriated her even more, and she hit my window angrily. *Thud!* I looked at the supplies on the passenger seat and considered a bribe but decided she was way past a chocolate frog. Even after she walked away, I was too scared to get out. When I arrived at school later that morning, a colleague asked me about a social media post in our local online newsletter.

'Hey Sue, is this your car?' She swivelled the computer screen around as I walked into the workroom. Medusa had posted a close-up image of my car, with registration number and a less than flattering description of me, for all to see. I stared at the screen. I'm not a prolific social media user and wasn't aware of the neighbourhood newsletter in which I now featured. I was both embarrassed and slightly unnerved. The day wasn't getting off to a good start, and the bell for recess hadn't even gone.

After work, I drove around to the police station for advice on dealing with the post, hoping my mum or the kids hadn't seen it. The police officer shook his head. 'Why do people have to do this stuff?' he asked, more to himself than me. By 'people', I assumed he meant the ones who spat Pollock-style vitriol on car windows and posted awful things on community newsletters, not the ones who over-enthusiastically made way for the elderly. I resisted the urge to clarify because it crossed my mind that he must meet a lot of Medusas in his line of work. To my relief, the post was removed, and the police rang to say they'd spoken with the person involved, describing her as 'one of our more belligerent residents'.

If this had happened a year earlier, I would have reacted differently. I might have ignored her until she went away and then gone about my business, relaying the story in a 'Guess what happened to me today?' kind of conversation. I would have said something along the lines of, 'There was this angry woman at the supermarket who carried on like a pork chop because she had to wait a few extra moments in the car park.'

A year earlier, I might have simply waved her away and driven off. I might even have got out of the car apologetically and tried to smooth things over. A year ago, I might have done any of these things, but at the time, she may as well have been wearing combat gear and carrying an AK-47. If you can picture a full-blown gorgon with poisonous snakes for hair coming at you with a gun in the supermarket car park, you get some idea of where my head was at. I felt like a sitting duck. It rattled me and left me feeling unsafe for weeks afterwards. When the image of my car and registration details were shared for all to see, it felt like a violation over which I had no control. I told myself it was safer and easier to avoid going to the shops and took to sending James a list of things to pick up on his way home instead.

When I shared my Medusa story with a colleague, he told me about an incident of a more threatening nature involving his wife. In a fit of rage, another driver caused significant damage to their car while she was still in it. Other motorists had filmed the incident, so they reported the person involved, who had to pay restitution for the damage he caused to the car. However, there was no restitution for the damage caused to my colleague's wife, who, like me, was left feeling scared and intimidated. Thankfully, the post in my community newsletter was removed, and I doubt anyone would have cared too much anyway. But I did. It mattered to me that someone could scream at me in public, hit my car window, and publish my personal details. For a long while, this incident reframed the way I went about my daily life. Volatile and aggressive behaviour exacerbated through the screens of social and mainstream media, and no doubt exacerbated by my paranoia at that time, had a diminishing effect. In an effort to stay out of harm's way, I shrank further and further within myself. But my fear was a clever foe. It sniffed out and prised open the cracks, exploiting the areas where I was exposed until I had little to shield me from the damage it caused.

Fear found me again not long after my run-in with Medusa, when I went for a walk after school, as I often did to clear my mind. Staying well clear of the supermarket, I headed in the opposite direction to a nearby park. As I got closer, I became aware of a disturbance near the playground equipment involving a group of local teenage boys. It was a nice park, but you had to pick your times. Early afternoons were best because parents brought their children there to play, but in the late afternoons, the local lads gathered, and there were occasionally scuffles accompanied by some rather choice language.

I recognised a troubled young man I'd encountered previously when several students had reported someone was menacing them as they walked home from school. The assistant principal and I had gone to investigate and undertaken several weeks of after-hours yard duty, which I referred to as 'guard duty', after the boy in question ripped a plank of wood from the fence and used it to threaten students. A nail-studded fence post had the potential to do a lot of damage, something I thought about as I watched for my children, who walked home through the park too. Although the young man was known to police and had been revolving in and out of the youth justice system for quite some time, it seemed there wasn't much they could do. We hadn't seen him around for a while, and I'd heard rumours that he'd moved out of the area. But here he was. Convinced that if he recognised me, he'd bash me senseless, I put my head down, quickened my pace, and gave the boys a wide berth.

To minimise the risk of further venomous interactions, I avoided the supermarket car park and took to locking the doors whenever I got in the car. Now I avoided the local playground too. I became hypervigilant in my avoidance of snakes in all their different forms. I saw all these kinds of people as predators who operated with a survival-of-the-fittest mentality. I was a long way from being at my fittest and felt like easy prey. With an almost instinctive need for self-preservation, I hid, avoided drawing attention to myself, and, whenever I sensed danger, ran as fast and as far as I could get.

On our many adventures to Australia Zoo when the children were little, I'd listened to a young Bindi Irwin trying to convince us how beautiful snakes are. In up close and personal encounters, the kids reached out and stroked scaly bellies as snakes slithered over their handlers, peering a little too closely for my liking into their small snake faces. They watched in fascination as their tongues appeared to lick the air.

I'd tried hard, for their sake, to overcome my fear of snakes, hoping we could all become brave Wildlife Warriors like Bindi, but sadly I failed to see snakes as anything other than an animal to be avoided at all costs. The knowledge that they were more frightened of me than I was of them is all well and good, but I don't sink my fangs into people and inject them with toxic venom when they get too close—although it must be said, it has merit as a self-defence technique.

Learning to tread carefully and to avoid the snakes in my life— the reptilian and human kinds—was a skill I'd perfected out of pure terror. I didn't feel safe, physically or emotionally, so I was even less willing to walk among them in case I inadvertently stepped on one. For four years, I operated in a heightened state of flight and didn't stick around long enough to discern which ones were poisonous and which ones were harmless because to me, a snake was a snake was a snake, and every one of them was a threat.

CHAPTER 10
SIDELINED

Although I was still experiencing moments of panic, they were milder and becoming less frequent. Having received my initial diagnosis, I recognised them for what they were. I was more attuned to both the symptoms and the after-effects: the brain fog, memory loss, and the inevitable feelings of uncertainty that descended. While shadows still plagued me more than twelve months after the episode, the dark days I encountered were less severe. However, Michael was about to suffer a bitter disappointment, and when he did, fear and dread raised their fists and slammed me back into the broken blessing my life was becoming.

Every parent knows it's so much harder to watch our kids deal with life's storms than to weather them ourselves. When they are suffering and feel lost, we would gladly take it all on to spare them the torment, but life doesn't work that way. As hard as it is, their lessons are theirs to learn, and watching them deal with disappointment, with failure, can be an agonising process. As it was for me when Michael, then in Year 10, applied for an overseas cricket exchange, along with two of his mates—for which there were only two positions. Three friends. Two places. The boys were in class together when the news came, and Michael watched as the successful candidates were both called to the office to be informed of their selections, returning to class celebrating their success. Michael was called out last and delivered the bad news, but by then, he knew he'd missed out. And he was gutted.

For an adolescent boy who defined his identity through sport, this sport, it was a cruel disappointment, brutally received. Nobody had intended it to be that way, but there it was. And when our kids receive a knockout punch and are down for the count, they need the people in their corner to be strong, calm, steady, and rational—everything I wasn't—to help them get back on their feet.

He rang me from school after receiving the news, and with the sickening feeling that comes when you hear your child breaking, I left work early to pick him up. The urgency I felt was not so much in getting him but rather getting *to* him. When I did, he was a forlorn figure in a slumped school uniform—a brave face holding on—which made me love him even more. He looked up as the car pulled into the pick-up zone, and I wanted to get out and hug him tight the way I did when he was little. But he was a boy in a man's body now, and I'd learned to hug him with my heart.

'We'll get through this,' I said with more reassurance than I felt. I knew he didn't hear the words, but I hoped the sound of my voice might break through. His tie choked him, and he wrestled with it, yanking it off. When we got home, he chucked his school hat away, and it landed in the pool as we made our way into the house, an act of teenage defiance in response to an overwhelming disappointment. It floated, a sodden, felt-grey statement of rejection.

'Fuck them!' he said.

'Fuck them,' I agreed. I cursed in solidarity with him and said it with gusto. Hearing his mother use the F-word would leave him in no doubt of my allegiance. But it was a wasted F because he didn't notice.

Jumpy and agitated, he paced the kitchen. This was a sign I recognised, and an alarm bell went off somewhere inside me, perhaps warranted, perhaps not, but instinctively I didn't let him out of my sight. Unsure whether to follow him around or give him the space he needed to hit out at the world, I scrambled for words to take the hurt away and bring him back, but they hung uselessly in the air between

70

us. I heard his breathing as heavy and hard as his disappointment and wanted to soften the blow with every maternal nerve. We sat mutely until he said he wanted to get away, go mustering up north with his cousins.

'I can't breathe here, Mum,' he said miserably.

His school phoned, but I didn't pick up because I didn't want to leave him alone. I texted James, who was working in Toowoomba, two hours away.

Can u come home? He understood everything I couldn't say and knew intuitively he needed to come home for both of us. The school phoned again, and this time I answered.

'I don't know how to help him,' I said.

'Neither do I,' said the deputy principal, who was sympathetic and keen to reach out. Having raised children of his own, he felt the weight of having to make a difficult decision. I tried to talk Michael out of the flight response, which was all too familiar to me, but he wasn't ready.

****

In the few weeks that followed, I became two people. I tried to be a pillar, to hold him up when he swayed, but it took all my effort, energy, and focus. I would steel myself when he came home to make sure I could guide the hurt, which turned to anger, which turned to self-doubt. We reminded him of his goals and encouraged him to make plans for achieving them, but it was a battle to keep him plugged in to anything because he didn't see a clear future. We tried to stay firm and maintain the boundaries he now pushed against, like staying at school, knowing it would be a mistake to give him an easy 'out'. We tried to find a balance between allowing him space to be upset and reminding him that our expectations regarding the way he conducted himself hadn't changed. As a family, it was a time of crisis, and I wasn't my best self.

I tried to still the quiet panic I felt bubbling away again, but the shadows of my inexplicable fear resurfaced. Behind closed doors, I was falling apart, dodging people again. I avoided conversations about my kids, or anyone else's, and the situation at home invaded every waking moment. The head shakes came back—a physical gesture to short circuit the cycle of overthinking that took hold. I cried constantly and found myself in different rooms in the house with no idea what I was doing there. It was Groundhog Day, and I was cast adrift once more, sucked away from life by the dangerous undercurrent of an obsessive and unrelenting sense of foreboding.

I became short-tempered at school, partly because of sleep deprivation and partly because the sadness had caught me all over again. I felt the whirlpool gathering speed, threatening to drag me under. I was pointedly dismissive in a meeting one afternoon, fed up with bureaucracy that I saw as both time-consuming and at the bottom of my priorities. Knowing I'd snapped at the messenger, a kind and amiable messenger, I was ashamed of my rudeness.

Shame on you, I chastised myself.

For God's sake, get a grip.

Not you again, I hissed at the voices that had re-emerged. *Piss off.*

And so, the battle raged.

My response was disproportional to the event. We'd supported the kids through disappointments before and were ready for more. Relationship break-ups, losing grand finals, missing out on jobs, failing exams—as parents, we knew these were in store and felt prepared for them. Rationally, I knew working through the messiness of life built grit, and I stepped back occasionally to allow our kids to experience the maelstrom of life. Yet again, I was thrown off guard by my inability to work through this with a sense of perspective the way I'd previously been able to. And I felt an added urgency to pull myself together, to be what my son needed.

My duality was difficult to process on a cognitive level and disconcerting, to say the least, on an emotional level. During the past thirteen years that James had been working in the corporate sector, he had taken on increasing responsibility at work, which meant more of the day-to-day parenting fell to me. As his job demanded additional time and frequent travel, I gradually covered more of the 'at home' jobs. I supervised the kids' homework, found overdue library books, and tested them on spelling words. I timed their speeches and practised home science experiments. I put my foot down when they asked to do, watch, or wear something that wasn't appropriate. The point is, as they were growing up, I saw myself as their go-to person, the one who tried to guide them through the pitfalls of early adolescence. I knew on a daily basis which way their teenage worlds tilted; I mediated disputes and read their moods. In short, I had proximity. But now, I was failing as a parent when I most needed to be a good one. I was letting the team down, not only as a parent but as a partner as well.

The kids knew from a young age they couldn't play one of us off against the other. Despite the need to work away sometimes, James always reinforced my parenting decisions. He spoke to the kids on the phone each night when he was away. When he was home, he made sure he was a presence. He coached Michael's cricket team four years in a row until Mike diplomatically suggested he might want to let one of the other dads have a turn. He watched Cate's gymnastics class whenever he could and caught up with the other parents at netball.

'Dad and I are a team,' I reminded them if, on the very rare occasion, they wanted to test the strength of his parenting in absentia or asked me to keep a misdemeanour from their father. Up until that fateful Saturday morning mind-snap, we'd always co-captained, making family decisions together. We backed each other up even when we had different views on how to handle the kids. 'Mum and

I are a team,' they'd heard all their lives. Except now we weren't, because one side of the team was sitting on the bench and the other took on the role of head coach. Rightly or wrongly, I felt sidelined as I watched James step in to help Michael deal with the hit. It was hard to be benched in a game that really counted. One I'd trained for all my adult life. For the good of the team though, I knew I had to let James call the plays for a while.

James grew up playing rugby league in Goomeri, a small outback town in the South Burnett. His childhood afforded him the freedom that comes with growing up in the country, something that has continued with his sister and her husband, who live with their four daughters on a family cattle station in the Gulf of Carpentaria. Our kids have benefitted from many outback adventures with their cousins, embracing station life, unencumbered not only by the restrictions of their own suburban lives, but also free from my watchful eye. After a couple of visits up north, I had to accept that just as I'm not cut out for camping, I'm not cut out for life in the outback either. In Gulf Country, it's an even bet the kids are swimming in waterholes with crocs washed in during the wet season.

Try as I did, I never became comfortable washing my hair in water that runs as muddy brown as the Norman River. However, this isn't something kids notice, and they eagerly went mustering, often camping along the way and swimming in the dam. They even entered various rodeo events where once Cate came first in the junior calf ride and won a trophy, fifty dollars, and most importantly, bragging rights.

They ran around in bare feet and heard language that made their ears pop. At night, they slept in swags underneath a blanket of stars, which shine more brightly out there than I have seen anywhere. The air is clean, and the earth underneath them feels solid. The peace that comes with sleeping beneath the outback sky is what we call Big Sky Time, which is where Michael instinctively wanted to run.

The harsh realities of outback life—drought, flood, and isolation; puppies who've come off second best to a deadly brown snake; the remains of a stillborn calf; stock horses struck by lightning in the wet season—instil a pragmatic resilience. It was what I saw in James the first day we met—he was grounded, perhaps by country I hadn't known and didn't yet understand. But he did. He understood the oppressive heat and deluge of the monsoon is short, that bruised, punch-drunk skies of purple-black give way again to diamond nights.

He understood, in a pragmatic way, that the storm would pass for Michael. But my emotional state seemed inexplicably linked to my son's. Michael's birth had not been easy—he came into the world, suddenly and surgically, by emergency caesarean. When he was delivered, the obstetrician invited James to cut the umbilical cord. I wonder whether, in that symbolic gesture, their relationship had been defined differently from the very beginning. While James was able to separate himself from Michael's experience, I was not. My emotions mirrored his, connected somehow by a force stronger than me. *Can mothers ever separate themselves emotionally from their children?* I asked myself.

By this stage, we were struggling to keep Michael at school at all. We spent a long night sitting in the kitchen, trying to work out how best to support him. I hugged a tepid cup of tea and noticed how the markings of our lives had turned our wooden table into a historical family artefact. Of homework reluctantly completed and documents signed, of shopping lists and party invitations. Etched in the timber were half-formed words from when the children were learning to write and pressed too hard on the paper. The table even bore the marks of Michael's baby teeth, the mystery of which we've never been able to solve.

It resembled a weathered map, worn with years of use, and I thought back to my ill-fated geography lessons in high school, where Sister Matthew, old-school and stubborn, was doggedly determined to teach me about contours and topographical maps. Despite her efforts, I've never been good at reading maps, but how I wished I could read this one now—the one that charted the touchpoints of our lives so far so we could more easily determine which direction to take.

We started with what we knew—Mike was a sociable, outdoorsy kid who loved being active, and the less time he had to stew over missing out on the exchange, the better. Luckily, James is also sociable and has a wide and eclectic mix of good mates. After a few phone calls, we had a plan that went roughly like this—put Michael in the way of good men, and wear him out with hard work. After a whole night of brainstorming, that was pretty much it.

He undertook work experience for a welding company in Toowoomba, where he spent his days in the sweltering heat of the workshop listening to advice from the older guys on the floor, who told him, in rather colourful language, to stay at school so he had more choices than they did. Tick.

He went up north to cattle country, where our brother-in-law had him work long, hard days building a work shed, and came away knowing they would not support a proposal that allowed him to drop out of school. All his cousins would finish school, and so would he. Tick.

He attended an agricultural course in Longreach, Central Queensland, learning horsemanship and working with livestock. Under the supervision of course leaders who were experienced in mentoring young people, he met like-minded kids from surrounding stations who invited him to jackeroo when he'd finished school. This gave him something to look forward to. Tick.

In addition, James booked three weeks annual leave, and together they planned a road trip through the Northern Territory. They pored over maps, discussed tyre widths, which swags to take, and what kind of weather to plan for. The trip was exactly what Mike needed and became a boys' epic adventure, featuring several unsung heroes who, although they didn't know it at the time, were the map we needed.

Among the people they stayed with were Haynsey, the owner of a cattle property who enlisted Mike's help with mustering on four-wheel drives, and Gibbon, who took them exploring around Darwin and Kakadu. They drove on to Katherine and went fishing with another mate, Kim, who took them up in his light aircraft for an aerial view of the spectacular Katherine Gorge. It's hard not to be inspired by country like that, and when Kim handed Michael the controls mid-flight, it opened yet more possibilities. He was outside every day, working alongside no-nonsense, practical, well-grounded men with a get-on-with-it approach to life. The plan worked, and without knowing it, they helped point him towards a future he liked the look of, and he found his feet again.

Throughout most of this time, I remained on the sidelines. The actual implementation of our plan fell entirely to James, as did the practical need to take enough time off for an unexpected road trip through the Red Centre. Uncomfortable with my new and, hopefully, temporary position on the bench, I felt a mixture of relief that James had our boy and guilt that I didn't.

When we scraped together the deposit for our first home just before Michael was born, a very modest three bedder, James was nervous about our ability to service the loan on his then-teacher wage, which seems laughable given the price of real estate now. At the time, I reassured him he wasn't taking it on alone, that we were a partnership, and he could rely on me to contribute too.

Now, I felt like I reneged on that deal. One day when he found me crying, he tried to provide some perspective by reminding me gently, 'No-one has died.'

'Then why does it feel like someone has?' I asked.

****

Friends who've had broken bones describe a weakness that remains, even after the bone has healed. They remain conscious of the break and instinctively protect it from stress. Sometimes, even years afterwards and despite rehabilitation, it aches, or arthritis develops, and they feel it may never be the same again. I wondered if my mind was broken in the same way, prone now to relapse. Would I ever completely heal, or would I fracture emotionally every time things got rough?

For the next few months, my husband watched us for different reasons. Michael recovered quicker than I did, and he found his way again. I floundered for a lot longer, held back by shadows made even darker by my lack of perspective and the voices that seemed to be forming a permanent groove in my head. My grandmother used to tell me that her aching joints could forecast the cold. Now I wondered if my tumultuous state of mind was an indicator of more stormy times ahead.

And how did all this affect Cate? On the day I picked Michael up from school, she came in through the gate with her backpack slung over her shoulder and stopped momentarily at the sight of Michael's hat, half-submerged. As children of schoolteachers often do, she knew there are some questions you're better off not asking. Instead, she saw what needed to be done and scooped her brother's hat out of the pool without saying a word.

James and I were married at Sacred Heart Catholic Church in December 2000.

Great mates. Michael (2 yrs) and James in 2004.

Upside down as usual. Cate reading in the kitchen.

A trip to Fraser Island. This photo captures both the kids' loves at the
time— cricket and cartwheels.

Preparing the cricket pitch. My pot plants came in handy as fielders.

Michael mustering in Gulf Country.

James has always had my back. Here we are riding a scooter on my birthday.

Cate and I watching a local rugby match in England.

Me standing on Westminster Bridge in front of the London Eye just
before the UK went into lockdown on 23 March, 2020.

James and I at the Trevi Fountain in Rome. When Europe gradually came
out of lockdown, there were very few tourists. The lack of crowds was a
silver lining to travelling during the pandemic.

CHAPTER 11
HOPE

Perhaps the reason I felt like someone had died was because the old me was gone. The person who laughed freely and often, the person who gleefully planned staffroom pranks, seemed like a ghost of the past. The best part about plotting an elaborate stunt was implicating others in them, like the time I persuaded my colleagues to convince our deputy principal that he'd poisoned the staff. We had parent-teacher interviews scheduled until 8.30 pm, so he'd arranged catering for the evening meal. Over a few whispers during dinner, I'd teed up half a dozen teachers to call in sick the following morning. The deputy principal and I carpooled, so I was perfectly positioned to make sure the sting went as planned. As I got into the passenger seat, I remarked that I thought I had a touch of gastro. The seed was planted.

Five minutes later, he received the first call. The teacher was very sorry, but they wouldn't make it in because they were feeling unwell. He made a mental note to call in a relief teacher when we got to school. A second call came in a few minutes later. Someone else hadn't slept because they'd been up all night 'vomiting' and wouldn't make it in. They apologised for the late notice. He made another mental note. A few minutes later, another call. The plan unfolded beautifully.

'Hmmm …' I feigned concern. 'That's unusual. There must be something going around.' I turned and looked out of the window to hide my grin. Another call came in. And another. I went in for the kill.

'I hope it's not food poisoning from last night,' I said, placing my hand over my stomach. He went a little bit pale, and I momentarily hoped I hadn't overplayed it. Undercover work is delicate. As he parked the car, I threw caution to the wind and pushed a little further. 'I wonder if we should notify the health authorities?'

He took the stairs two at a time. As he entered the administration building, he saw all the staff who had called in sick, doubled over with laughter and flopping against the wall in hysterics. Slowly he pieced it together and almost collapsed with relief. We all laughed together—the loud, contagious, conspiratorial laughter that had people shouting over each other to explain their part in it. We laughed so loudly that people came out of their offices to see if everything was okay.

****

In the weeks and months following my Saturday morning breakdown, I lost and grieved for the person I used to be. By the end of 2017, the old me who relaxed easily in the company of others was nowhere to be found. I used to laugh so hard telling a funny story that I couldn't get to the end of it; my kids would roll their eyes and say, 'Mum's lost it again!' Michael has perfected the 'Mum laugh', which he uses in good-natured mockery of my hysterics, and to my great amusement, Cate has inherited it.

In the depths of my illness, that all disappeared, and I sorely missed the company of shared laughter. Where was the person who made up silly awards for her colleagues or hid chocolate frogs in random places around the school? I missed the old me who planned an anonymous treasure hunt for a colleague just shy of retiring, a man who tried to hide his marshmallow softness behind an oft-grumpy persona.

Despite fooling some of the younger classes, I loved him to bits. As he followed the clues I'd left throughout the day, he found his treasure—a new lunch box with a beer inside to replace the old ripped supermarket bags he usually used. A man needs to approach retirement in style, after all. I missed being the person who took risks, who didn't sweat the small stuff, and above all—way above all—I missed the warmth of joining in.

When I'd named grief as my growing-up fear at the sleepover as a kid, I didn't imagine it would be myself I'd grieve for. During this time, my closed body language must have made me seem miserable and unfriendly. I no longer joined in conversations with my colleagues, and I'm ashamed to say I didn't bother to get to know the new teachers at my school. I showed no interest in others, and as a result, I became distanced from them. If I had spare lessons throughout the day, I went home so I could avoid the staff room.

As a mentor, I'd always enjoyed tapping into the energy and commitment of new teachers, watching different styles evolve, and the relationships with their very first classes grow and strengthen. Over time, they established their own routines, gradually trusting themselves enough to let go of textbook theory in favour of the personalities of the kids in front of them.

Helping young teachers navigate school processes, working out the value of people over policies, had been a source of joy to me. My work in this area had been recognised just two years earlier, in 2015, as a finalist in the Excellence in Teaching Awards, held in Brisbane. Their notes and thank you cards, affirmations of our work together, lie in a vintage tin in my cupboard at home. They are reminders of the lucrative returns on investment when new teachers transition successfully into the education profession and their first classrooms.

Now, I had very little energy or interest in mentoring. In fact, I actively avoided it because I knew what I'd bring would be half-hearted and ineffective. Worse, my demeanour might dull the vibrancy with which they immersed themselves in their new careers. This put me at odds with my values.

Once, in a job interview, I was asked how I felt about being in conflict with others. I'd replied that while it was uncomfortable, I found it preferable to being in conflict with myself. Now, I seemed to be permanently conflicted, jumping from one emotional spot fire to another, trying to stamp out the flames of guilt, which flared every time I said no to helping at a school activity. Surfing for the Disabled? No. Vinnies sleepout for the homeless? No. Valentine's Day chocolate wrapping? No. Relay for Life? No. Mooloolaba Triathlon? No. Women of Strength Program? *God* no!

Each time I said no, it meant somebody else had to say yes. Inevitably, one of my colleagues put their hand up to fill the void. There is an amazing degree of goodwill and generosity among teachers. Despite the profession becoming more corporatised, teachers continue to see their work as a vocation, and there are high levels of collegiality in most schools. My colleagues willingly volunteered to take on a host of extra-curricular activities—mine as well as theirs. They accepted my excuses at face value—the children had something on, we had visitors from interstate, I had a truckload of marking to do—and waved away my apologies good-naturedly.

We'd adopted the expression 'swings and roundabouts' and used it to mean that everyone's turn would come around eventually. We went about our work with an understanding that people jumped on and off the extra-curricular roundabout, volunteering their time as they were able, depending on their circumstances. But I could see the roundabout had become lopsided—that my colleagues, especially some of the younger teachers, were doing the lion's share of the work.

I was embarrassed about not pulling my weight, so I built a wall of self-preservation to keep people at a distance. I did a good job of making myself unavailable, and gradually, people stopped asking me to be involved. The cooling of my connections with others made me feel lonely, and I staggered around in that loneliness for too long because I didn't know how to begin the thawing process that would allow me to feel their warmth again.

And so, it is quite surprising that a clear memory of Wednesday 15 November 2017 emerges as a reminder that there were some gems amid the gloomy days that invaded me. I was working part-time, and I didn't need to go into school until late on Wednesdays, so after I'd dropped the kids off, I headed to the beach for a mood-boosting power walk.

Striding out along the esplanade with my head down and earphones in, breakfast radio served the same purpose as daytime television, escapism. The newsreader announced the results of the two-month postal survey on same-sex marriage. Australians had voted in favour of marriage equality. Not only that, but eighty percent of the population had voted of their own volition, and every state and territory had voted YES. For reasons I don't fully understand, the impact of this news on me was profound.

Rather than avoiding eye contact, I smiled at people who walked past me, wanting to stop and say, 'Hey, have you heard? We voted yes to same-sex marriage!' I didn't stop strangers in the street, but I did bounce back to the car, and on the way home, I called in to The Cheesecake Shop on Aerodrome Road. I bought a huge multi-layered rainbow cake, as sweet and colourful as the result delivered just hours before.

That night, James and I sat around the table with the kids, celebrating what I felt had been a hard-fought victory for people who'd lived in the shadows of inequality for too long. While the kids were happy with the result, they weren't elated in the same way I was, and I suspect, like many young people, their musings centred more around why this was still 'even a thing'.

What was it about the decision that lifted me from despondency? It was something more than simply the recognition of justice. After a year of feeling disconnected and isolated, this was a rare moment of connection as the country cried out in a contagious emotional outpouring of relief, solidarity, and love. That night, with a belly full of rainbow cake, I fell asleep anchored by a deep sense of calm that came from the conviction that we'd got it right. We'd taken an important step towards ensuring our young people would grow up in a fairer and more tolerant world.

While this memory is proof of the periodic reprieves from the anguish I felt, they were more like the hopeful clicks of a pilot light than full ignition and didn't last long. Paradoxically, it was the classroom that restored me when I found myself in the doldrums on the days when it was hardest to go to school. The warmth of the students' energy and humour carried me, at least temporarily, away from my struggles.

There have been days throughout my career when I haven't enjoyed being a teacher, but not one when I haven't enjoyed teaching. Although the pressures and demands of *being* a teacher were taking a toll on me mentally and emotionally, the *process* of teaching acted as a salve. The statement, *I am a teacher*, had become a heavy one, laden with the bureaucratic demands of the job as defined by policy makers, politicians, the media, and society in general.

As a teacher, everyone seems to have an opinion about what you should be. In contrast, the statement 'I teach' felt more life-giving, more dynamic, just so much more doable, and I found the hijinks and the melodramas of a high school classroom addictive. Each young person is their own unique character, and teaching is like living in the pages of a choose-your-own-adventure story.

A seemingly inconsequential lesson comes to mind as an example of how the theatre of the classroom warmed me. It was a noisy lesson, typical of that class, who were forever keen to test their ideas. As their thoughts blew through the room, they created a whirlwind of learning, which gathered momentum, and I had to work hard to keep up.

That week, we were watching examples of performance poetry. I asked if anyone would like to share an example they'd found, and a boy shot out of his chair to put his example up on the screen. He moved like a rocket, and as he took flight, we all got swept along, waiting to see where his new knowledge would take us.

He was prepared for that moment, but none of us realised it was coming. For the next three minutes and forty-one seconds, we were mesmerised by a performance entitled 'Emmett', performed by a team of young Philadelphian students during the Brave New Voices poetry finals in Atlanta. I say mesmerised because the class hung off every confronting word.

We felt every nuance and rode every lilt and anguished expression. So powerful was the performance, it was almost difficult to breathe in the silent seconds that followed. No-one moved; no-one spoke. When this happens in a classroom, when time stands still and everybody instinctively respects the space, you know they've lost themselves to something that might change them.

Again, the 'rocket' claimed control of the class and led us into a deeper understanding, as he explained the poem's historical context and the definition of the word 'lynched'. The poem lit a flame in him, and as his words tumbled out, they ignited the classroom. His passion wrapped itself around us and carried us into the world of Emmett Till, 1955, Mississippi, and the ugliness of racism.

I hovered, ready to jump in and fill in the gaps, take questions, lead the discussion— contextually, this was a long way from their own experience. As I scanned the room, though, I saw the class was looking directly at our young teacher, giving him permission, and I knew my job was to get out of the way and let the learning unfold.

From the back of the room, I nodded my encouragement, and as I watched him fly, I felt my quiet acknowledgement that despite the challenges I was facing, there were days like this when I felt I'd chosen the best profession in the world. As I stood at the back of the classroom witnessing his triumph, something within me stirred ever so slightly. Something warm and brave and strong. And right there, I felt the power in my profession—the power in teaching. Our days are full of little miracles that we don't expect, and yet, we find ourselves standing in the middle of them. When I got home and my kids asked me what happened in my day, I answered, 'Magic. Magic happened.'

Even the classes that threatened to derail often left me smiling. This was the case during a spelling lesson when it became apparent almost immediately that the troops were restless. This can happen sometimes because underlying peer issues are bubbling away or simply because blood sugar levels are low.

On this day, I suspected it was the weather, as we'd had a spate of hot, humid days. Outside, dark clouds were heavy with empty promises; inside, the classroom was heavy with … what? I couldn't quite put my finger on it. All around us, the country was either crippled by drought or drowning in flood, and the classroom is not immune to the effects of climate change. It was a hotbox, a pent-up calm before a tropical Queensland storm, and I felt the potential volatility in the room. Two boys prowled like author Linley Dodd's rapscallion cat: two young Slinky Malinkies, covertly avoiding their work.

They were loveable larrikins, but I knew their tomfoolery would not be well received by their peers, who were hot and bothered. Everyone's tolerance levels were low. Eventually, when I couldn't ignore it any longer, I said to the more restless of the two, 'You've been wandering around all morning, mate. What do you need?'

'I need a stapler. Do you have a stapler, Miss?'

'What do you need it for?'

'Well, I can't concentrate because my shirt pocket got ripped when I was playing tiggy. It keeps flopping around, and it's paranoy-ing me.'

'It's what?'

'Paranoy-ing me. You know, when you get paranoia?' I smiled. If only he knew.

'I see. Well, if I find you a stapler and you fix your pocket, do you think you'll be able to concentrate on your work?'

'Mmm.'

'Ok, but only one staple, not a whole row of them.'

I handed over the stapler and added the word *paranoid* to our spelling list, wondering how his mum would react when she had to de-staple his shirt. For a while, he was settled, and a hushed stillness filled the room, but then, while returning the stapler, he reached out and flicked his partner in crime. It was a quick flick-and-run, which was just enough provocation to avoid real trouble and to bring on the histrionics he knew would follow. If we could have watched it in slow motion, it would have resembled one of those scenes from a David Attenborough documentary where lizards with super-fast tongues lash out and a hapless fly is stuck on the end before it knows what's hit it. In this case, the hapless fly pretended to be too dumbstruck to move.

The simple too-fast-for-the-human-eye wrist whip was genius. A guaranteed crowd pleaser and welcome entertainment to break up the monotony of a spelling lesson. The victim feigned injury, and the perpetrator, a chameleon in more ways than one, feigned innocence. *Here we go*, I thought, bracing for impact. Sure enough, full of false indignation and holding a non-existent flesh wound, the flickee shouted, much louder than necessary,

'Oww! He just hit me! Miss, did you see that?' All heads looked up. I let out an inaudible breath and took note of the distant rumble of thunder, warning me to keep a lid on the drama. In our part of the world, we just never know when the skies are going to open and pelt us with hailstones before we've had a chance to duck for cover.

'I did indeed,' I responded quietly. 'Are you alright?' Still smarting from being chastised for a minor misdemeanour earlier in the day, he seized the opportunity to lessen his transgression by bringing someone else down, and his mate would do. There is no honour among twelve-year-old thieves, especially hot and bothered ones.

'Well, aren't you going to consequence him?' His tone dripped with the accusation of favouritism. I bought myself valuable time by adding the word consequence to the list on the board.

'Yes, I am,' I replied seriously. With the voice of mock authority, I issued a declaration to the flicker, 'Prepare to be consequenced!'

The class smiled at my misuse of the word. Thankfully, the guilty party, placated by the not-half-bad repair job he'd done on his shirt and satisfied by the fact he'd caught his fly, didn't care two hoots what his consequence was. He completed a token punishment of picking rubbish up off the floor, grinning at his mate as he did so. Once he'd paid his penance, the show was over, and both boys settled back down.

This brief, comical performance provided the class with a slight reprieve from the oppressive heat, and until the bell went for lunch, the storm clouds that had gathered inside and outside the classroom were held at bay. Nobody even noticed I had added two more words to the spelling list. I walked out of the classroom, and while I avoided the staffroom and headed home to hide instead, I felt a flicker of warmth in the knowledge that despite the paranoia going around, we had all left the room smiling.

When I enter into learning, real learning, as opposed to simply giving kids something to do, I can get lost in it, much like I imagine a conductor can be carried away by an orchestral composition. Literature, like music, consists of different genres and lends itself to interpretation, which means it's never enough to simply teach the notes—the goal is to teach the rules and then show students how to break them. To let them play with language and develop an appreciation and love of the art itself so that it stirs something within them—something that whispers to their childhood and calls to them far beyond their school years.

This is why my junior English classes always start with reading—readers are born when stories meet a deep yearning of the human spirit. The students are used to the routine, choosing a book from the yet-to-be air-conditioned school library. On what was shaping up to be a particularly sticky afternoon, four girls cornered me in a little reading nook between Action and Adventure, and Science Fiction.

'Look what we found,' said a voice from the huddle, holding out a freshly date-stamped book, now valid for another fortnight. Leaning in, I asked, 'What am I looking at?'

'Alliteration!' she said triumphantly.

'And listen to this,' said her friend, reading dramatically. '"My heart is thumping like a drum". That's a simile.'

'The sun enters the room like an unwelcome guest,' read another.

'Check this out: "a burst of orange … that bled out like a sunset".'

Wow, we agreed. These are wonderful similes and fantastic images. I fist-pumped myself on the inside.

Back in the classroom, I watched as they were lured into different worlds. When students are fully engaged, you can feel it; I could almost hear the synapses connecting as I moved quietly among them. Some were immersed in futuristic worlds, others lauded heroic victories. Others wandered through romance or lamented an untimely demise they didn't see coming. Their tastes were wide and varied.

Suddenly, one of the boys sat straight up, gripped by something he'd just read, his eyes the size of small plates. He absorbed learning like a sponge, soaking up ideas, growing them until he found a place to plant the seeds of his new knowledge. I knew it was only a matter of time before this kid grew something important for the world. He saw that I'd seen him. I put my finger to my lips and gestured, 'Shhh.' He knew the chance to tell me would come, and although his eyes shone, he didn't break the magical silence of the room.

When reading time is finished, I always ask, 'Who wants to tell us about their book?' Most of the hands in the room go up. In this class, there were still some who didn't enjoy reading, and I found myself hoping that I'd be able to give them this gift before the end of the year. I chose 'the sponge' before he imploded.

'Anh Do's uncle was laid in a coffin in the morgue, *but he wasn't really dead!*' He whispered this, the thought of being buried alive too terrifying to say out loud.

'O-M-G, that is like my worst nightmare!' someone said, and for a minute, they talked about what you would do if you were buried and not really dead. This idea was too awful to contemplate and led to further discussion about what if. One by one, they described their books—the suspense, the heartbreak, the narrow escapes, the human tragedies, and the triumphs of their adolescent heroes.

In the back corner of the classroom, a girl, a natural leader with the enviable combination of being both curious and clever, was hooked by a dystopian novel where the stories of people's lives were told in pictures tattooed on their skin. Used by a totalitarian regime to control social order, strangers read each other's ink, summing up one another in seconds.

The students were at an age when tattoos were noteworthy. Until recently, the teachers at our school had to cover their tattoos, but as the word 'diversity' gained traction, this requirement had softened, so the teachers' tattoos were a topic of interest. The class discussed what tattoos they would choose and why. Some of the more conservative kids were adamant they'd never get one, while others with older siblings thought they were 'cool'.

The idea of becoming walking illustrations of our choices, good and bad, was food for thought. Having tattoos as permanent public records of our lives led to a discussion about the value of our privacy, our personal freedom. I suggested this was a discussion the author wanted us to have, repeating my mantra that good literature always leaves us asking more questions.

'This is why certain regimes over the centuries have tried to restrict reading, to ban books,' I said. 'It's hard to control people who ask too many questions.'

'Is that why the Taliban shot Malala?' There it was from the middle of the room. Real-life connection.

'Who shot who?' The classroom buzzed as the ones who knew filled in the ones who didn't, who looked to me in disbelief as if to say, *Can this be true?* When the buzz settled, the reader of the dystopian novel explained that when people died, their skin was removed and made into books, which became a library of human archives—a library of warnings. The thought of skinning people was a bit off-putting, so the discussion turned to another person's book. They put 'dibs' on the good ones and discussed them in much the same way they talked about the latest Netflix series. Sometimes they said, 'Miss, you *have* to read this book; you would *love* it!' Sometimes they brought in books their parents had read when they were teenagers. To them, they were 'just reading'. But I knew their books were the vehicles through which they would learn to think bigger and ask better questions. They would build empathy as they shared the protagonist's emotional journey in overcoming adversity. They would safely experience universal themes—survival, hope, tragedy, and triumph—through the pages of someone else's story. Later that week, I noticed one of the girls had borrowed *I am Malala* from the library. I almost danced to my next class. I didn't, but I wanted to.

It was, and still is, a luxury to get lost in learning that is not assessed against syllabus criteria and for which I am not bound to report. During these precious, free-reading minutes, I don't have to assign a grade, collect data, analyse, or measure reading growth. There are no assignments or exams. There is just the room and the space we create each day to read. In this space, the kids learn to play with the notes and be carried away by something that stirs them to ask questions, to seek meaning.

Echoing the words of children's author Mem Fox, who'd been my lecturer at teachers' college and whose passion for literacy had rubbed off on us all, when I tell a child to read, I want it to sound like chocolate, not like medicine. Some days, reading for the fun of it feels like the last bastion of my English classroom—the one piece of the learning paradigm that hasn't yet been swallowed up by data metrics—and I guard it stubbornly.

When reading time was over, we studied a poem entitled 'Annie McClue' by talented performance poet Murray Lachlan Young. It's about a little girl who doesn't flush the loo. The kids laughed, and they critiqued the performance, identifying effective techniques they might be able to incorporate into their own performances. After some discussion, I said, 'Let's move on to example number two.'

Slight pause.

'Number two ... get it?'

'Ooooh, gross! That's lame!' They groaned.

'No pun intended,' I said, emphasising the word 'pun', which we'd been learning about. We then looked at an example of slam poetry.

'It's like rapping, but without the music,' I explained. They experimented with their voices, playing with the rhyme and rhythm of the poem. Some of the boys picked it up quickly, and their bodies moved instinctively to the beat. They had the street moves down pat, and as they found their groove, I couldn't help but be caught up in the dance too.

CHAPTER 12

NO WOMAN IS AN ISLAND

By the beginning of 2018, I'd felt a thousand little deaths and felt like I'd seen a thousand more. But I'd had a thousand awakenings too. Although I didn't recognise it at the time, these painful little goodbyes, the letting go, cleared the way for tentative new understandings as my consciousness shifted. Teaching had cautioned me not to take things too much to heart, but in a fragile state, the thick skin I'd developed peeled away in layers.

In high schools, where students constantly test the boundaries, I sometimes felt vulnerable and exposed. To provide context, most interactions I'd had with students where boundaries could have been crossed were innocent blunders. Largely they were my fault due to rookie errors in my early years of teaching. But some had been more sinister and had left a lasting impression on my feelings of safety at school.

For me, there's a big difference between a calculated manoeuvre designed to cause harm and a heat-of-the-moment exchange. I've been on the receiving end of quite a few hot tempers and been outsmarted by agile, streetwise kids who had the upper hand. I learned a thing or two about communicating with teenagers as a result.

'Who died and made you queen?' snapped one young lady, bristling at my teacher-tone when I'd obviously pushed too hard.

Her words were like a whip, and soundly rebuked, I took off my crown, adjusted my tone, and tried again. On another occasion, during a uniform blitz on untucked shirts, I scraped the egg off my face after stupidly repeating something I'd heard an older teacher say.

'If you boys don't tuck your shirts in, I'll come over and tuck them in for you!'

Of course, when they grinned at each other and invited me to do so, I turned bright red and had nowhere to go but back into the staffroom, leaving them to high five each other with shirts hanging down around their hips. It was a clear win to them, and any thoughts I'd had of disciplining them for a uniform violation followed me and my pride into the staffroom.

A light-hearted crack that brings a laugh at the teacher's expense is par for the course, as one of my male colleagues found out during an all-boys sex education class. As he wrapped up the lesson, he thought he'd done a good job of steering the discussion.

'Boys,' he said, 'sex with someone you don't know very well is overrated.'

The room was quiet for a few seconds until one of the boys quipped, 'Are you sure you're doing it right, Sir?' The class collapsed with laughter, and he walked out of the room admitting defeat.

His story reminded me of my own sex education classes as a student, when a male prac teacher suggested that sex before marriage was no different to test driving a car.

'Girls, you wouldn't buy a new car without test driving it first,' he said. 'Why would you get married before you've had a chance to test drive your future husband?' In those days, we still spoke in assumptions. In my Catholic high school, the thought of test-driving boys like we would test-drive a car was scandalous. Outrageously, irresistibly scandalous. Which made him outrageous and irresistible, especially as he was under twenty-five, unmarried, and wore jeans to school.

'Wouldn't mind taking him for a test drive,' said one of the girls who had older sisters and was already frequenting the clubs in Hindley Street. She began singing 'Jump in My Car' by the Ted Mulry Gang whenever he walked past.

'Mmm-mmm jump in my car, ooooh I wanna ta-ake you home.'

Soon, the song followed him around the school as other girls joined in until Sister, who no doubt realised the boundaries were too close to being crossed, called us together for a girls' talk. She reminded us sternly that none of us were old enough to drive just yet, and Ted Mulry was banned until further notice.

Every teacher has these mostly harmless, often comical, career-shaping moments in which they are bested. Mine made good fare for stories about my early years of teaching. Taken in isolation, I was able to maintain a healthy perspective around unpleasant interactions at school, knowing you must take the good with the bad in any job. But occasionally, I miscalculated the cumulative psychological impact of more serious interactions—both on me and on other students who were left feeling vulnerable.

When you're a student working alongside a peer who is impulsive, aggressive, intimidating, or just plain mean, it can be an uncomfortable place to be. While I established expectations and classroom rules early, and sometimes displayed them colourfully around the room, this didn't prevent them from being broken. While I intervened, deflected, and imposed consequences, I couldn't ensure everyone followed the rules all the time, and the students knew it. In theory, schools should be places of learning where everyone feels respected and able to participate in a safe and inclusive environment. I can repeat the theory ad nauseam, but it doesn't always hold up in practice, and not surprisingly, it doesn't mean much for the student, and at times the teacher, who feels unsafe at school.

As I became more experienced, I picked up more easily what students sometimes call 'bad vibes'. When, as a more seasoned teacher of about ten years' experience, I walked into a senior class, I felt bad vibes almost immediately. There was a tangible discomfort in the room, but I couldn't put my finger on why. One of the students from the class approached me from behind and gave me a hushed warning.

'Don't sit on the chair,' she whispered, just loudly enough for me to hear the fear in her voice. I stayed well clear of the teacher's seat, choosing to facilitate the lesson from different vantage points. After the students had gone, I pulled out the chair. It was littered with thumbtacks, pointed side up—tiny, sharp middle fingers literally sticking it to the teacher. It wasn't the thumbtacks I found unsettling—in fact, I was reassured by the perpetrator's lack of imagination—it was the fear I'd heard in the student's almost inaudible warning. The need she felt to protect me. From what? From whom?

It dawned on me that the girls in this class had learned to be careful. Something was going on in that classroom, and the half-hidden warning indicated that no-one felt they could call out whatever it was. If I'd been able to find out, I hoped I would have been brave enough to show them how to do it, but I was never able to get to the bottom of it and never shook off the toxic feeling in that classroom.

I could deal with in-your-face teenage backchat, even open hostility that was recognisable for what it was, but occasionally, shadowy interactions that had me questioning whether they were even happening felt more sinister. They were subtle and elusive, and I became more alert and more conscious of my personal safety at school.

Even as an experienced teacher, I felt uneasy when I became the target of stalking behaviour by a senior student. He was a secretive boy and found it difficult to make eye contact. When I dismissed the class, he was slow to pack up, always the last to leave the room. One day, after everyone had gone, I noticed he'd forgotten his hat and went to take it to the lost property pile. Underneath the hat was a drawing of a large black penis. This was nothing new in high schools, where penises, which seem to draw themselves, appear in all manner of places. So why did I feel uncomfortable when I looked at this particular artwork? Why did I feel like it was intended for me?

At the end of the next lesson, he packed up slowly and was the last to leave the room again. He didn't overtly linger, but it was getting awkward. I began dismissing the class differently. I allowed the boys to go first as frequently as I could without accusations of favouritism. But then, he would hover at the bottom of the stairs that I used to get to my next class. Soon I began noticing him when I had yard duty. Was it just coincidental that he seemed to be turning up more often? Perhaps it was just my imagination, but it didn't feel like it, and I was relieved whenever he was absent.

I thought I'd put a lid on these kinds of experiences. I thought I'd pushed them safely into the perspective of the past. However, more than a year post-diagnosis, I felt the familiar uneasiness when a game of mixed basketball turned sour in the final countdown.

I'd inherited a PE class because the sport teacher needed to leave school early, and my name was on the list of covers for the day. Having devoted my formative years to ballet, I'd managed to avoid sport and knew nothing about basketball. I didn't know the rules, I didn't know how many players could be on the court at the same time, and I didn't know when to blow the whistle. James was a trained PE teacher, so I asked him for a quick soldier's five and repeated the drill before I left home.

'So, I blow the whistle every now and then and call out "travel" when the students are running without bouncing the ball?' He nodded. It made me feel more uneasy than I did already because it was based on the premise that students who don't know me will obey a whistle.

'And do this.' He moved his arms around each other in a roly-poly motion.

'Really?' I asked doubtfully, raising my eyebrows. 'Is that what your HECS debt paid for?' I remembered the hours I'd spent at uni drafting and redrafting essays—in the days when we wrote them by hand. I practised the roly-poly move and hoped this would be enough to get me through a forty-five-minute lesson—thirty-five if I allowed five minutes change time at either end.

'And don't say bouncing—say dribbling,' he called out as I tucked a wad of poetry papers under my arm, feeling doomed.

Luckily for me, when I met the class in the gym, one of the girls was wearing a knee brace and couldn't play, so I made her chief referee. She was a sporty kid who knew what she was doing, and the game got off to a good start. For coast kids who are raised on team sport, a game is never just a game. The primary school had banned lunchtime handball due to the too-frequent fisticuffs over hotly contested rules about 'linies' or 'double bouncers'. Likewise, a friendly game of basketball became a matter of life and death as they vied for victory.

I could smell the hormones and sweat, which, as a non-athlete, I was never too sure what to do with. As the game gathered speed, a boy sprinted down the court to the hoop, creating a wind gust as he zoomed past me.

Geez, mate, it's not the Olympics, I thought to myself.

'Travel,' the ref called, blowing the whistle. But he went for it anyway, leaping up and dunking the ball.

I knew someone would ignore the whistle. I looked at my watch. The referee moved toward the centre of the court to bring the play back, and from somewhere in the middle, one of the boys yelled out to his mate, who still had possession.

'Give it to her—you know she wants it.'

And with that, a simple cover lesson for me, and a fun basketball game for them, got messy. At a time when my life was messy enough and I wasn't dealing with life's muck very well. I looked at the ref, whose face was already set in a way I recognised and understood, and the same uneasiness I'd felt years before caught up with me. It caught her too, as she stood in a spotlight of humiliation, not knowing what to do or where to look. She was rooted to the spot—exposed and vulnerable. Susceptible. When I looked at her, I saw myself. What happened next was the result of reflexes sharpened by my own past experiences rather than mental acuity.

I walked into the spotlight and stood next to her, putting my hand up for the ball. The game had come to a complete stop, and I called them in. There was no need for a whistle now.

'So … who said it?' I asked, holding the ball out of play. We'd all heard the comment, but this wasn't my usual class, and I couldn't reliably pinpoint the source. Silence followed as they looked down, some with their hands on their hips, others prodding at the discomfort with their feet.

'If you own it, you can put it right. But if you don't, then I will have to put it right.' To them, I was taking back control of a game. However, I felt I was taking back control of something more important. I tried to keep my tone neutral because if it sounded like a threat, I would scare the young man into denial, and I wanted him to own up. After a few more uncomfortable seconds—the time it took for him to work out that it was in his best interests to confess—a quiet voice said, 'It was me.'

His face was stricken with the knowledge that he could be in a whole world of trouble but didn't yet know if he was. I sent the rest of the class to the change rooms while I had a tough and potentially awkward conversation with a student I didn't know. I had about three minutes to determine whether what he'd said was out of character or whether it was a pattern. I fished.

'If you could press replay on that game, would you do anything differently?'

'I know, I know. I'm so sorry—as soon as I said it, I knew.' I studied his face. Some kids are truly sorry, and others are truly sorry they got caught. In this case, he was an older student who knew very well he'd crossed the line, and his face told me he'd felt the damage. I accepted his regret because shame teaches kids nothing, and some of them can be too hard on themselves.

'Yes,' I said with a nod, 'I think you are. I'm going to stand right here and watch you make that apology to the person who needs to hear it. Make sure it's a good one.'

It had been a long time since I'd had an instinctive response that I trusted. It had been a long time since I'd stepped into the spotlight instead of shrinking away from it. It was simultaneously a stepping in and a letting go of previous shadowy encounters I'd walked away from. For the first time in over twelve months, my instincts felt right.

Being a lazy teacher is easy. I know this because I've been guilty of it. I've looked the other way on hot days and pretended not to see contraband water pistols. I've been blind to forbidden nose rings, and I've even ignored a few sneaky peeks at a neighbour's test paper, knowing the students who need to look at other people's work need all the help they can get. It would have been easy to pretend I hadn't heard the comment on the basketball court. It would have been easy to blow the whistle, brush it off, and send the class on their way.

There is a term in teaching called 'tactical ignoring', which simply means picking your battles. As a teacher, I've never felt the need to win every battle. In fact, sometimes, I purposely let a few go through to the keeper. But even on my bad days, when it took every ounce of willpower to get to school, I wanted to win the most important ones. Even on my bad days, I knew the game would be up if they didn't matter anymore. That is why when the documentary about Aboriginal AFL player and 2014 Australian of the Year, Adam

Goodes, *The Final Quarter*[6] went to air; I used it as the basis of a class study.

****

Adam was booed relentlessly for three consecutive seasons in football stadiums across the country. The ugly behaviour among some of the football crowd at that time was confronting viewing. Adam's story made me squirm emotionally, and in the public debate that followed its release, it seemed many others squirmed too. For a while, the truth of our country was difficult to hear amid the deafening noise that erupted on our television screens. As he shone a spotlight on the impacts of racism, Adam Goodes became vulnerable to the insidious booing he endured game after game. It impacted his mental health to the point that he walked away from football completely. He remains disconnected from the game he once loved, declining an invitation to be inducted into the Australian Football Hall of Fame.

Although Adam's story is very different to mine, it resonated strongly for several reasons. The scene in the film when a young Collingwood supporter called him an ape reminded me of how I'd felt when Medusa spat her venom—violated. I watched Adam trying to hold on to a professional career he loved, one he'd devoted his life to, one that in many ways defined who he was. Football was a big part of Adam's identity, just as teaching was a big part of mine. Like Adam, I was also trying to hold on to a professional career I loved and had devoted my life to. The kicker was knowing that if the crowd could turn on Adam Goodes, week after week, with a whole country watching, then the crowd could turn on me too. The crowd could turn on any of us.

As an educator, even one who wasn't firing on all cylinders, I was uniquely placed to effect change by empowering young people.

Teaching allowed me to put stories in their way that were worth knowing about. It allowed me to introduce them to battles that were worth winning so that hopefully, they would have to endure fewer of their own.

The boys in the class who played club football were hooked. As we watched the documentary, I was buoyed by their responses and reminded of the capacity of young people to hear the truth and name it.

'Why do all these voices belong to middle-aged white guys?' came one question. And another, 'Notice the people who shout the loudest are the ones who've never experienced racism?'

Their own stories of racism were confronting. Whenever the topic of racism was raised in class—almost without exception—the students shared their personal experiences of degradation. Of being called terrorists, of being asked if they eat their pets, of their parents being taken for the cleaners of the businesses they own. Some had been told to get back on the boat; others had been accused of being dirty, dangerous, or untrustworthy.

Their stories reminded me that, as human beings, we are intricately connected. Our human fragility overlaps so that my truth, as every social movement across every generation has shown, cannot stand separate from that of my brother or my sister. In the 17th century, English poet John Donne captured this in his essay, 'Meditation XVII', when he wrote, *Any man's death diminishes me, because I am involved in mankind.'* This is where I found myself—diminished by mankind's little deaths. As their stories collided with mine, I died, just a little, for every student who'd been told they didn't belong. And I died a little bit more as Adam's story became a personal one.

****

An uncomfortable awakening grew within me. I say 'grew', but in truth, it gnawed at me, as I acknowledged that I'd never had an authentic conversation with an Aboriginal person about their personal experience. Professional protocols had largely enabled me to avoid it.

While I'd participated in programs that sought to create a deeper appreciation of Aboriginal culture, the First Nations leaders we invited into our schools came in the capacity of guest speakers. They showed us traditional artefacts and shared the Dreaming stories of our region. They spoke to us of ancestral customs and the creation story of the Rainbow Serpent. I knew that my local area of Maroochydore was named from the word *Moorookutchi-dha*, meaning a place of black swans. Each year, we took our junior classes to the banks of the Maroochy River, where we sat beneath the shade of a huge camphor laurel, listening as Uncle Lyndon Davis, Gubbi Gubbi First Nations elder, taught us about the seasons and the local flora and fauna.

On school boards, I'd discussed how we might make education more accessible to Aboriginal students and improve retention rates. In our efforts to Close the Gap, we celebrated NAIDOC (National Aboriginal Islander Day Observance Committee) Week and observed an Acknowledgement of Country before formal school assemblies. But had I side-stepped sensitive conversations, guided, and in truth protected by policies of political correctness? I had little real understanding of Aboriginal experience beyond history, Dreaming stories, and sporting legends.

Adam said, 'If there's something you don't understand, let's talk about it.' How could I open such a conversation, and with whom? What if I ripped a bandaid off a 200-year-old wound from which our Aboriginal peoples are still trying to heal? The scars are deep, and it didn't feel like a good time to be taking bandaids off when I was lancing abscesses of my own. But Adam's voice kept whispering to me, and I wondered whether a painful conversation was better than no conversation at all.

Despite my trepidation, I approached a friend and colleague, an Aboriginal woman who'd also seen the documentary, and asked if I could talk to her about it. These were new conversational waters for me, perhaps for both of us, and together we waded in. She talked about growing up in a white family, never knowing her mother. She shared the humiliation of being followed by security in our local shopping mall. She spoke as a child of the Stolen Generations, with the pain of not knowing country. Telling her story is hard, not only because it is a hard story to tell, but because she feels it needs to be delivered carefully.

'We don't have the luxury of getting it wrong,' she explained. 'When we talk publicly about what it means to be an Aboriginal person in this country, we have to get the tone just right. If we sound too defensive, or too angry, or too emotional, people stop listening.' Then she added, 'And it's important for me to get the tone right for the next Aboriginal person who works here.'

Listening to her experience changed my sense of self, just as watching Adam's story had. I'd heard her story, not those of the ancestors or the Dreaming, but her personal story as an Aboriginal woman living on the Sunshine Coast. She raised her children, played with her grandchildren, worked in schools, shopped, went about her life the same way I do, except differently. Through her story, I was awakened more keenly to the painful legacy that we live with.

After work, I recounted the conversation to James.

'What does it say about me that today, for the very first time, I had a real conversation about Aboriginal experience?' I asked.

He thought for a moment before replying, 'It says that it's never too late.'

'I'm finding out it's never too late to learn a lot of things lately,' I said. As one of the students wrote in their paper about *The Final Quarter,* 'School can change a person.'

Donne was right—*I am involved in mankind.* I am intrinsically connected to my brother and my sister such that their deaths diminish me. No woman is an island. And no man is either, which is something I'd discovered by teaching boys and learning more about their emotional fragility too.

CHAPTER 13
BOYS AND ME

When I first began teaching, I wondered, *What impact can I, as a woman, have in teaching boys to become good men?* As I witnessed people gather in the flickering candlelight of street vigils, such as the one held in Kangaroo Point, Brisbane in May 2018—mourning innocent lives lost at the hands of unspeakable domestic violence—this was a question I asked myself more often. According to Mission Australia, one in six Australian women experience violence by an intimate partner.[7] In addition, statistics published by Lifeline Australia reveal that seventy-five percent of Australians who take their own lives are male.[8]

As a female teacher, I have always felt that the role I played in the lives of boys mattered. I felt compelled to play whatever part I could in helping adolescent boys develop a strong sense of purpose; form respectful, authentic relationships; and contribute responsibly to the community. Being an impactful teacher of boys was instrumental to my work, and for me, it was fraught.

I attended a Catholic girls' high school in Adelaide, where, with the exception of a handful of girls who crossed North Terrace to study physics at Adelaide High, we didn't hear the voices of boys in our classrooms. My high school education was mostly delivered by independent, no-nonsense, celibate women who seemed unflappable. They were gentle women with a faith that enabled them to stand their ground with calm, demure determination. Under their guidance, shaped by the motto *'veritas'* (truth), I heard the rich stories of scripture—of martyrdom that transformed human experience—stories that nudged me closer to a better understanding of my own truth. Many of us had brothers, but mostly I thought boys were annoying and tolerated them when I had to.

I began my teaching career with little understanding of the psyche of adolescent boys because of this chasm in my experience. I also was not prepared for their physicality.

I underestimated their fragility, their need to learn from lived experience, and their forays into impulsive and risky behaviour. I underestimated the emotional sensitivity of boys and their need for men to help them build a strong sense of themselves, just as my female teachers had done for me. In the grip of rapid hormonal changes, with testosterone levels through the roof, pubescent boys tested their growing strength at every opportunity. I sometimes found teaching boys tough, not less rewarding or less joyful, but the challenges were different simply because I see the world through a female lens.

I felt on more familiar ground with girls. Growing up, I'd learned to identify the eddying waters of girl behaviour. Eddies can be dangerous—they pull people under if they gather too much momentum—but I'd learned to recognise when they were gathering speed. As a teacher in the classroom, if I couldn't stop the swirling waters of the girls' cliques completely, I could at least slow them down. Dealing with boys was different. I watched for rogue wave after rogue wave as the roughhousing of boys—who underestimated the strength of their growing bodies—got out of hand and became outright brawls. Boys took greater risks, which put them in greater danger, which, in turn, demanded more of me.

As a pre-service teacher, I was ill-equipped to intervene with a young man in my English class whose risk-taking had already led to heavy drug use. He stared vacantly from the back of the room as the class discussed the lyrics in Midnight Oil's song 'Beds are Burning', a protest song about the forcible removal of the Pintupi people from native land. It was an empty, drug-fuelled gaze that I had been too slow to understand.

'He's stoned,' one of the other boys explained to me one day.

'He's what?' I asked naively.

'Stoned. You know, strung out. From drugs. That's why he doesn't remember what we do in class.'

I didn't know. The antics of my school days were limited to wedging a cigarette between the lips of Our Lady, who stood reverently on a balcony outside our Year 12 common room. We hid to watch Sister's face as she looked up and saw the Holy Mother smoking. And she only ever smoked cigarettes—Winfields; none of us would have dared turn up to school stoned.

My four-year degree had taught me how to adjust lesson plans for ADD, ASD, and ADHD, but it hadn't covered LUI—Learning Under the Influence. I knew very little about drug addiction. I did the best I could and referred the student to my supervising teacher, but the gaunt, almost haunting look in his eyes would prove to be a constant reminder that I wouldn't be able to help them all.

I recognised the same look when I ran into an ex-student around Michael's age, who'd dropped out of school. He looked tired and haggard underneath his hoodie—and much older than his sixteen years. The chubby, cheeky face I knew was gone, and as we talked, he self-consciously pushed his hands deep into the pockets of his jeans. When I asked him how he was, he replied, 'Not great,' and looked away, gazing faraway into the distance. Perhaps at a past that felt further away than it really was. I was glad he stopped to say hello and was happy to see him, but I was heavy-hearted too. I questioned whether I'd been able to make any difference at all and felt like I was no closer to saving teenage boys from themselves than I'd been as a pre-service teacher.

As a female teacher, I sometimes felt ineffective when dealing with sensitive boys trying hard to fit into the world of men. Kyle* was one of many boys I taught without many men in their lives. A lot of my students lacked male role models—sometimes because of family separation and sometimes because their fathers worked away. Added to this, the feminisation of the teaching profession meant most of their teachers were women. When Kyle ran away from class one day and I saw some of the other students looking cagey, I asked the teacher next door to keep an eye on them while I went to find him.

He was leaning against an out-of-bounds tree trunk in an overgrown area known as 'the hideout'. It was a strip of bush bordering the back of the school oval, and it was popular because the kids knew the teachers would rarely clomp through the long grass to chase them back, especially if it was a lady teacher with nice shoes.

'Ky—there you are. I've been looking everywhere!' As I got closer, I could see he'd been crying. He scooted his bum around to the other side of the tree so I couldn't see him. Unfortunately, I had to clomp through the long grass.

'Mate, you're supposed to be in class. What's going on?'

'Nothing.'

'Well, obviously something's happened to upset you. Maybe I can help. Why are you out here by yourself?'

'Coz I'm a loser,' he said, shuffling around the base of the tree away from me each time I got too close. I glanced down at the dry leaves, the dirt, and the twigs on the ground, hoping I wasn't about to sit on a soldier ant. We sat in the shade, on opposite sides of the tree, knowing that the trunk of an old gum would not provide refuge from adolescent shame and humiliation but sitting there anyway.

'I asked Anthony* to ask Ruby* to ask Skye* if she'd go out with me, and he said she said she would, and then I went and asked her, and she said no in front of everybody, and now everyone knows.' The story bumbled out in a rush. I understood, better than I could let on, how he felt. I'd run away from the thought that everyone would know, too. I was still running. He paused for breath before adding, 'People think I'm a loser, and I get everything wrong.' I heard his shoe scrape the dirt as he shifted beneath the weight of adolescent angst. I wanted to say, *Hey, go easy on yourself. You're supposed to get things wrong when you're only twelve.* Instead, I said, 'It took courage to ask Skye out. You're trying hard, and you're honest. These are the marks of a good man.' But I suspect he needed to hear it from a man.

Whenever I questioned who I was, which was frequently throughout my self-imposed isolation, I looked to the other women in my life for inspiration. I watched my female friends who, from my perspective, lived their lives like warriors as they ran households, cared for elderly parents, and undertook additional study often while working fulltime. They not only remained true to themselves but found time to support each other too.

I remembered the example set by my teachers and mentors: generous, smart women who lived their lives with grace. Through their example, they showed me what was important. Who did Kyle have to show him? I understood that he wasn't hiding from me, or the girls, or the other boys, but from his own self-doubt. I understood it better than he would ever know. But understanding it was one thing—being an example to him was another, and I couldn't help but feel my words would have meant far more coming from a man.

****

There is a random spontaneity about boys, which has been a great source of entertainment and perplexity to me over the years. Raising a boy of my own gave me some insight into the way boys reach out and touch something just because it's there. As happened one evening, when we meandered slowly back to our hotel during a family holiday when Michael was twelve. Along the street was a row of cactus growing in large rectangular planter boxes, and I warned the kids not to touch them, as they would get a nasty sting. The words were no sooner out of my mouth than Mike reached out and put his finger on the end of one of the spikes, receiving a sharp prick for his efforts.

'Ouch, that's sharp!' he yelped, recoiling in pain. We all turned to look at him.

'Mike,' I said incredulously, 'I just told you the cactuses are sharp! Why on earth did you do that?'

'I don't really know, Mum. I just wanted to see for myself,' he said, trying to shake the sting out of his hand. As he looked closely at his finger, searching for the minuscule pinpoint of his injury, Cate laughed her head off.

'Idiot,' she said. 'Mum just told us not to touch them.'

Serves you right, I thought, and as we all laughed at his pain, I captured the moment. It's one of my favourite photos of his childhood—his expression is a declaration of boyhood and all that comes with it. It's also a reminder that when I give boys a warning, it often acts a catalyst. Most boys needed to learn the hard way, which made teaching them harder too.

Teachers make, on average, about four decisions every minute,[9] and I reckon some days I cashed in almost my whole quota on the boys. When the going was tough and I had to drag myself into school, I dealt with their antics by counting to ten, and by good fortune rather than good management, they didn't hurt themselves too badly under my watch.

I managed to get one down from the roof when he'd shimmied up a drainpipe to retrieve a lost ball. Another played chicken with the blades of a ceiling fan, poking his fingers between them, unperturbed by my protests that they could have been chopped clean off. Walking from one lesson to the next, I was almost decapitated by a pair of size ten school shoes and looked up to see a boy hanging from the rail of the second-floor balcony—his mates timing how long he could hold on before losing his grip. I even saved one lad from suffocation after an experiment gone wrong saw him squashed into a vacant locker. When his friends realised that none of them knew the combination, they panicked and came running into my classroom to raise the alarm. Why did he do it? He just wanted to see if he'd fit.

Boys test their female teachers just as they test their mothers. And since I couldn't meet them on the same footing as their male teachers, I sometimes had little option but to outlast them. This was time consuming and draining at a time when my emotional reserves were low. In one case, it took me a whole week to turn defiant refusal into begrudging acquiescence—all over a chip wrapper.

Yard duty is the teacher equivalent of the dog park; students run in every direction, and there are scuffles and yelps in the quest for dominance. The younger boys bounce and scamper like puppies eager to test boundaries. The older boys tend to roam in groups. Part of the deal with yard duty is to get them to pick up rubbish, a task I detested as much as they did because inevitably they argued that it wasn't their rubbish, so why should they pick it up. The idea that it's not their rubbish, but it is their school, doesn't catch on until graduation.

A small group of older boys hovered near some lunch tables— well-established territory that I was about to walk into. As I walked past them, I asked, 'Would you fellas mind picking up some of this rubbish and putting it in the bin just there?' I picked up some scraps too, and they went to it easily enough, plucking at the dry litter within their reach and avoiding the half-eaten apple cores and soggy banana peel the heat had glued to the concrete. Fair enough.

The leader of the pack didn't move, leaning instead against the bin with his arms folded. As the rest of us completed our litter sweep, we all felt it without letting on that we felt it. It was a clear challenge, a test by the pack leader whose territory I'd encroached upon. I knew if I passed the test, my life would be a lot easier. Conversely, if I failed and walked away, allowing him to not just ignore my request but refuse it altogether, I would have little chance of those boys following any of my instructions down the track.

I looked at him directly and, keeping my voice even, asked if he could reach a couple of chip wrappers squished between the gaps in the tables. Then I moved away, appearing to continue my rounds, so he had space to do it without me hovering over him. In teacher-speak, we call this 'take-up time', which loosely translates to 'saving face'.

On my second walk-by, it still hadn't been done, so I asked him again. He refused. My teacher instinct warned me—time and place. It was not the time or the place for a female teacher to take on a defiant teenage boy in front of his mates, especially this female teacher who was not at her assertive best. I would lose that battle for sure. Luckily, one of the other boys, a labrador-type, good-naturedly offered to do it instead.

'I'll get it, Miss,' he said jovially and bounded over to scoop out the chip wrappers with his fingers. I looked at him and smiled.

'Thanks,' I said lightly, disguising how I really felt—weary and worn out by the ones who made things harder than they needed to be. I kept walking but glanced back just in time to see the pack leader lift the bin and up-end the contents all over the ground. It was a very public 'Up yours!' and the boys who now guffawed and slapped him on the back knew it.

I desperately wanted not to have seen it. I desperately wanted to get through yard duty and go home. I desperately wanted to pass it to somebody else to sort out. But I knew it had to come from me. Allowing his year-level coordinator—a man—to step in would simply teach him that male authority trumped mine. I was on rocky ground with a boy who had high visibility—some kids are just known around the place—making it even more important for me to send a message about respecting a female teacher who'd made a reasonable request.

I met him at the beginning of every recess and every lunchtime for a week, and together we did litter duty. He barely said a word on the first day as we walked around picking up chip wrappers the wind had blown into shrubs and garden beds. Resentment emanated from every pore. Day two went much the same way, but by day three, I sensed a subtle shift. I guess he could only hold onto resentment for so long. On day four, he attempted to negotiate.

'We've done four days, and I've learned my lesson. Can you let me off tomorrow?'

'Nope. Good try, but a week was the deal.' He shook his head.

This wasn't about my need to win. It was about doing my small part to ensure that boys grow up to be decent, respectful men. It was about doing my job and still having the wherewithal to recognise the battles worth winning.

By Friday, the yard gleamed, and it was hard to find any rubbish at all. I'd earned a grudging respect by holding my ground. After that, he gave me a nod when he saw me at school, and occasionally some cheek to go with it. Because he had kudos among his peers, I earned some sway with the others as well and didn't have a problem with those boys who gave some of my colleagues the run-around. Still, it had been a tougher week than I would have liked.

****

Despite my best efforts, there were times when I felt that I didn't have the same cut-through as my male colleagues when dealing with boys. This was especially true in aggressive or violent situations. When I was teaching on the Gold Coast, some boys from my class ganged up on a student from another school while he was waiting at the bus stop. A member of the public who'd witnessed the incident and recognised the uniforms rang to report it, and the call came through to me. There appeared to be no connection between the parties—it was a random, impulsive act. The boys certainly felt my disapproval, but they didn't feel the gravity of their actions until they were made accountable by a man.

Having seen the positive outcomes in restorative justice approaches, we'd arranged for the students to make a personal, face-to-face apology to their victim on his turf, and I drove them over to the school. The ride over was silent, and again, I wondered, *What impact can I, as a woman, have in teaching boys to become good men?* A glance in the rear-vision mirror told me they were staring through the windows without seeing anything, but I resisted lightening their loads because I wanted them to sit with the discomfort of their actions for a while.

We were met warmly by the deputy principal, and as I introduced the boys, he looked them in the eye and shook their hands. I'm not sure what changed in that moment, but something did. We followed him into an office, where an older student stood up to greet us. My two sat down awkwardly, swallowed up by fabric-covered seats. They made quiet apologies and solemnly promised he would be able to catch the bus without fear of further harassment. I was struck by his dignity and was grateful and relieved by the way he thanked the boys for coming to make a personal apology.

'I know this wouldn't have been easy,' he said generously.

The boys talked more freely in the car on the way back to school. I congratulated them on the way they'd handled themselves and told them they'd earned the right to put it behind them. The whole interaction took no more than fifteen minutes, but it was an important stepping stone in paving the way for two boys to become better young men.

The moment a man with the right combination of gravitas and compassion extended his hand to my two young charges, calling them 'gentlemen', he invited them, by his example, to be more than they were. I felt an intangible shift in the air as though somehow, through that gesture, we'd entered into 'men's business'. I don't know whether it was the way he looked at them, the firmness of his handshake, something in the sound of his voice, but in that moment, they stepped up. And something instinctively in me stepped aside, knowing that I could not be as impactful as the man who stood in front of them—a man they'd never met before. I cannot model men's business. Boys need the men in their lives to do that.

What I *could* do as a female teacher was support my male colleagues, who intervened to change the trajectory for boys at risk. I'm not talking about abdicating my responsibilities here; female teachers play a vital role in shaping decent young men, but I felt it was important that male teachers entering the profession knew their worth and hoped they'd stay.

For a while, I was responsible for placing local and international students in my school to complete their practical training, and I observed an interaction between a young Canadian pre-service teacher and a group of middle school boys from his class. Will* spoke with a quiet intensity, and the boys listened with their whole bodies. He hadn't liked some of the language he'd heard them using around the school and was encouraging them to lift their game. We talked about the role he'd played and the impact of a life lesson coming from a young man with strength of character and personal integrity.

Will returned to Canada after completing his degree, but unfortunately, he decided against a teaching career, applying instead to the Canadian Mounted Police. When the recruitment officer contacted me for a reference check, I relayed the time in the classroom when he'd inspired a group of young boys to become better young men. I said I hope his chosen career would provide opportunities for him to work with youth because although Will had decided against teaching, he was a natural. I felt the loss, though, for all the boys he wouldn't teach.

CHAPTER 14
PAPERCUTS

'Can we swap cars for a while?' I asked James when I got home from school. The thought of driving around in his old ute wasn't appealing, but it was preferable to the alternative. He knew how possessive I was of my red Laser and that I hated driving his second-hand ute, which smelled of footy boots and Deep Heat.

'Why?' he asked, surprised.

'Because I had to suspend two girls for fighting, and one of their mothers told me she knows what car I drive.'

'Girls?' Physical fighting between girls was rare.

'Mmm. I was surprised too. Did you hear the bit about targeting my car?' I asked. 'I assume she meant with me in it.'

'Do you think she'd really do anything?'

'I wouldn't put it past her. She's mad, that woman. Can I drive your car until things cool down?' I figured she hadn't seen the ute parked at school and I could go incognito for a while.

'Sure,' he said.

This was my first taste of school leadership in 1998, during a contract as acting deputy principal in Rockhampton. The threat felt real because people did know each other by their cars. Since then, I've heard parents threaten to run down my colleagues in the street and witnessed an angry father stand over a staff member, warning if she confiscated his child's phone again—something the school policy required her to do—it would be 'the last thing you'll ever do'.

A string of harassing late-night phone calls to staff saw one principal inform an irate parent that he'd give her name to police if she rang any of the teachers at home again. I've been in staff meetings where we've been told not to meet with certain parents on our own and to copy line managers into email correspondence because unsubstantiated misrepresentations about teachers had brought them under question.

Unpleasant interactions with parents were not common, but they were not new either. I'd encountered unreasonable, out of control, and sometimes drunk parents at school before. These are often directed to more senior staff, and in previous leadership roles, I was used to defusing volatile situations. It almost always required a courageous conversation. In some cases, it meant standing my ground in the face of threats to vent personal frustrations to the media, initiate legal action, or make complaints to school boards. Some parents have even threatened to write a letter of complaint to the Pope!

During my career, I'd dealt with situations of this nature as an unpleasant but sometimes necessary part of the job. However, over time, the cumulative effect of witnessing aggressive interactions, watching as my colleagues were abused or threatened, chipped away at my emotional strength. Post-episode, my capacity to deal with difficult parent behaviour was diminished, making me more vulnerable to its impacts.

And it would seem I'm not alone. Peta Stapleton, Associate Professor in Psychology at Bond University, found over half of Australian teachers suffer from anxiety, and nearly one-fifth are depressed.[10] Furthermore, '… teachers are more susceptible to work-related stress, burnout and general psychological distress when compared to other occupations'.[10] A federal government inquiry in 2019 into the status of teaching heard that one in three Australian teachers leave the profession within the first five years.[11]

Alarmingly, according to a report by the Australian Catholic University, forty-five percent of principals were threatened with violence in 2018, and thirty-seven percent were attacked.[12] One principal stated, 'I've spent months at a time dreading the walk out to my car at night.' Another described the moment a parent 'nodded at a shotgun on their dashboard as they drove past slowly and looked at me'. Others report being headbutted, stalked, tailgated, and threatened with scissors. Yet another recounted a time when a parent 'charged at me, picked up a whiteboard in the foyer and threw it at me'.[12]

Speaking in an ABC interview about a report on *Teacher Targeted Bullying and Harassment* published by La Trobe University in 2019, Dr Paulina Billett, one of the leading researchers of the study, describes a teacher being threatened with a bow and arrow. 'They were told if they didn't leave the kid alone they'd get a bolt through the eye.' The story of a principal who was verbally abused at a school sports day brought to mind one of my school swimming carnivals. What should have been a day of friendly competition had us all on edge when a parent used their own stopwatch to check that we'd recorded finish times accurately, which in the case of swimming is to a fraction of a second.

Not surprisingly, the report found that the effect on teachers' mental health was severe, with respondents suffering symptoms of anxiety, depression, and PTSD, including panic attacks and uncontrollable shaking.[13] Parent bullying and harassment affected all aspects of a teacher's life, including their personal relationships. A large number of respondents reported needing psychological support. Most of the reported abuses were what researchers referred to as 'everyday incivility'. Noteworthy for me was the finding that '… it's the everyday little things that accumulate through the lifetime of a teacher's work, that erode the teacher's willingness to continue teaching'.[14] I wasn't there yet, but by 2018, after twenty-eight years of teaching, I could feel the glue losing its stick.

****

Teachers and parents all walk a precarious tightrope. Most of the time, we walk a rational straight line and manage to keep our balance, but sometimes the rope below us quivers. If it wobbles too much or for too long, we lose our balance, and the ground on which we land can turn out to be even less stable than the tightrope from which we've fallen.

When the ground shakes beneath you, it's unnerving. I'd experienced an actual earthquake in Christchurch in June 2011, when James talked me into a rare weekend getaway without the children. While we were waiting at the airport to fly home, a 6.0 magnitude earthquake struck. The young man who'd just served me at the café was there one minute and gone the next, diving under his counter before I'd worked out what was going on. He'd done this before—probably practised it during a workplace health and safety drill—but for me, as an earthquake novice, it was surreal. The lights above me swung alarmingly from side to side. Huge glass panels, which framed the view of the tarmac, seemed to bend and warp like the trick sideshow mirrors that distorted my reflection as a kid, magnifying the strangeness so the whole scene appeared like an optical illusion.

I lurched back to our table only to find James tucked away underneath it. For a moment, I wanted to laugh at the absurd spectacle of my husband hiding under the table, but as it dawned on me that everyone else seemed to be playing this ridiculous version of grown-up hide and seek, I took stock.

'What's happening?' I asked him.

'It's an earthquake,' he said, looking around for cues from those with earthquake know-how.

'An earthquake! An actual earthquake!' I repeated stupidly. Once my mind caught up with what was going on, I glowered at him. 'Thanks for coming to find me!' I said sarcastically as he scrambled out from under the table and reappeared rather sheepishly. I was conscious of a low rumbling that I couldn't place, but in the second, larger quake, which measured 6.5 magnitude, I realised it came from somewhere deep below the earth. A subterranean growl that made me look down to check the ground beneath me was still there.

Being on shaky ground metaphorically isn't that much different to being on shaky ground literally—the emotional ground on which you are used to standing shifts. As a parent, I've been on shaky ground plenty of times. I felt the rope quiver and spread through every part of my body in a simmering, violent rage when I found Cate scared and sobbing after being followed by the lolly man. The force of the blind fury I felt shocked me as I drove through the neighbourhood looking for a neatly groomed middle-aged man in a red hat.

I understand the parenting tightrope. I've slipped off it many times and have felt slightly aghast at what I may or may not have been capable of. Most of us are in this parenting thing together, this messy, wonderful, difficult, and joyful ride, working out the best way to do it as we go, falling off occasionally and giving each other some slack when we do.

I like to think the times when my footing faltered enabled me to bring a certain degree of empathy to parent exchanges at school, and for the most part, it did. In any case, many parents I've worked with are positive, warm, and have a healthy sense of humour, which makes the job so much easier. Most have a refreshingly candid understanding of their kids. This was true of one mum who affectionately described her daughter as head-strong and eccentric during an enrolment interview in one of the more inclusive schools I've taught at.

There are some schools where eccentricity doesn't fit. Schools, like towns, develop their own vibe and are not always accurately labelled. Some are viewed as being sporty or academic. Others are perceived as cliquey, and smaller schools especially can be seen as more personal. School culture varies, and in this school, I felt we could do eccentric. I was looking forward to meeting her because I seemed to connect with the spirited ones, and I did with this girl, who I came to think of as The Little Scorpion.

Her first year of high school went as expected, with a few tense moments along the way that had been easily massaged. As we neared the end of the year, I was glad to see that despite stinging some of the other kids occasionally, she'd made a good group of friends. However, one morning, she misread a situation after walking in late and assumed an injustice was being done to a quieter student in her class. She rushed to their defence.

According to eyewitness accounts spread on the grapevine via wide-eyed twelve-year-old gossip, she took on the teacher, and the situation escalated when she stood up and yelled, 'Why do you have to be such a bitch! You always pick on the shy kids, and you can't get away with it!' She stomped out of the room, slamming the door behind her, leaving the teacher and the shy kid wondering what on earth had just happened. Then she went underground to cool off.

We can overlook many misdemeanours, depending on the circumstances, but calling your teacher a bitch isn't one of them. If she hadn't used the B-word, I might have been able to plea bargain down to an apology, but she had, and there was no wriggle room in the rules for swearing at teachers. It warranted a phone call home, and she'd have to do an after-school detention.

I hesitated before picking up the phone because conversations like this could go either way. Some parents become overnight defence lawyers, backing their kids no matter what, and others will accept the school's ruling. In this case, Mum listened carefully to what went down and groaned.

'Welcome to my world!' she said. *'What am I going to do with her? I knew what we were in for as soon as she was born—she's a typical Scorpio!'*

I breathed a sigh of relief.

'Tell that teacher I feel her pain,' she said.

As I hung up the phone, I wished all parents could be so, well ... reasonable.

Perhaps there's a risk of hypocrisy in sharing the impacts of negative parent interactions, especially as the heat of my emotional responses reminds me that we've all been there. In the hundreds of interviews I've conducted throughout my career, I've seen first-hand the emotional distress of parents who are sleep-deprived, at breaking point, trying hard to hold it together for their children. As a parent, being on shaky ground at times is part of the deal, and we've all said things we don't mean. But when confrontations such as the ones I've described occur, everybody's sense of well-being is affected, and the research indicates that threatening and abusive behaviour towards teachers is on the rise. Kevin Bates, former Queensland Teachers' Union President, describes it as something that has '... reached a crescendo ... and needs to be dealt with'.[15]

I was still hanging in there, but I wasn't taking the knocks as well as I used to. When I found a young colleague in tears after a parent-teacher interview ended badly, I felt the tears of my own anguish congeal, a defence response to the hundreds of tiny papercuts of my profession, to the misplaced and sometimes relentless parent advocacy that undermined and devalued my work.

On the grand scale of things, it was a minor upset; interviews have ended in tears before on both sides of the table. Even as I listened while she tried to pinpoint where it had gone downhill; even as I sympathised with my friend, who gave up weekends and holidays to run workshops and spent hours planning lessons for the kids who find school hard; even as I knew how unfair it all felt—part of me also knew this parent had felt the irrational quiver of the ground shaking beneath them. They'd misstepped, reaching out instinctively to grasp at something that felt more solid by blaming the teacher. But still, papercuts sting.

Although it was a small tremor on the Richter scale of parent-teacher interviews, I felt the injustice of it more intensely than I should have, than I normally would have. Even though the injustice wasn't aimed at me, I couldn't shrug it off as flippantly as I had earlier in my career when I simply asked James to swap cars until the dust settled. I couldn't do what I'd done so many times before and which my colleague did now—pulled herself together and readied herself for the next interview.

'I'm okay,' she said stoically, brushing off the humiliation. 'It's fine.' As I watched her walk out into the dark for the night shift, I thought, *No, actually—it isn't. It really isn't fine.*

I wondered whether we would be able to keep her or whether she would join some of our other young teachers who'd resigned to travel or pursue other careers, having decided teaching wasn't for them. Ironically, I was the one who was being swallowed up by the statistics, unable to deal with the everyday incivilities that seemed to be invading school life.

CHAPTER 15
BUCKLING

Despite resigning from my coordinating role in 2017, my work in transitioning students into high school, and my interest in the middle years phase of education, meant that I continued in the school as a specialist middle years teacher. As such, I did a lot of work with students from grades seven to nine, not just in the classroom but also through pastoral programs. Having noticed the distressing impacts of rumour-mongering among the Year 7 girls, I facilitated a program at the start of each year, designed to target the spreading of rumours and gossip—and the troubling practice of trolling, in which an increasing number of girls were becoming ensnared. The activity was adapted from a scene in a movie which had been recounted to me by a friend.

Eight curious twelve-year-olds each held a small plate of flour. They stood in a circle around their peers. On the count of three, they blew the flour as far as they could over the group, and squeals of delight filled the room as the girls found themselves covered in a white cloud. It settled in the carpet around them, leaving faint outlines when they stood to brush themselves off. It turned their hair a comical grey, and for a minute or two, pre-teen old women giggled at the sight of each other. When the noise died down and the flurry of shielding themselves quietened, I asked them to gather it all up and return it to the plates. They looked at each other the way kids do when they don't understand an instruction but aren't quite brave enough to raise their hand.

'Can you pick it all up and put it back on the plates, please, girls?' I met their eyes and repeated the instruction.

'What?' they whispered uncertainly. 'Is she joking?'

They hesitated, wondering if their teacher had gone mad. But they were keen to please, and some of them attempted to brush the flour out of the carpet with their fingers. Clearly, it was an impossible task. After a few seconds, I stopped them, and when I had their attention again, I asked them to recall the last conversation they'd had. Could they recall the actual words that were spoken? Some sat easy and still, and others fidgeted a little uncomfortably, their body language giving them away. 'Is it possible to take our words back?' I asked.

Then I got them to describe what they'd noticed during the activity, and they replied that very few people in the group escaped unscathed. Even the volunteers got dusted when some of the flour blew back into their faces. They also noticed that some girls who were covered head to toe just happened to be sitting in the wrong place at the wrong time. A little cloud of flour hovered in the air, suspended for a few seconds above them all.

'What might have happened if we'd done this activity outside?' I asked.

'The wind would blow it further,' they said.

'Who knows how far our words might drift on the winds of social media?' I posed the rhetorical question knowing that many of them had received mobile phones to mark the rite of passage into high school.

****

The need for schools to instil values sits alongside the need to teach substance abuse awareness, resilience, driver education, the responsible consumption of alcohol, digital citizenship, cyber safety, and more recently, consent education. Some schools feed children because they come to school hungry. Mindfulness techniques, personal grooming, outreach activities, anti-bullying education, and domestic violence initiatives are just some of the pastoral care components being asked of our schools. Each of these programs has merit and seeks to address the issues our kids must be equipped to deal with. But when I consider the increasing demands placed upon schools to deliver such a broad range of programs, in addition to improving academic outcomes, I'm not surprised I buckled beneath the weight of our curriculum.

I've always loved the nitty-gritty of the classroom, where the kid factor is front and centre. I'm intrigued by the learning process and the challenge of working out how children think. Some are logical and methodical in their approach; they think in linear directions, stacking ideas one on top of the other, like building blocks. Other students construct thought webs that string and loop around them in increasingly intricate and complex thought patterns. If Rodin had sculpted a child version of *The Thinker*, instead of looking pensively downwards, seemingly weighed down by his thoughts, it would gaze upwards, reaching for ideas that, just like the stars, seem to be simultaneously beyond our reach and just at the end of our fingertips.

When children catch their stars, they shine in a way that is breathtaking to see. However, these moments were becoming fewer as my classroom became more and more test-heavy. Tests aren't much of a problem for students who perform well—they come into the room generally well prepared, and although nobody enjoys tests, take them on as a necessary part of school life. Some even enjoy the challenge and the satisfaction that comes with well-earned success.

This is not the case for the strugglers. They come into the room with faces and hearts set against what will likely be yet another failure. Many of the standardised tests tell them what they can't do rather than what they can, and as the frequency of testing increased, I watched them gradually stop reaching for their stars. Who can blame kids for disengaging with an education system that tells them time and time again what they can't do? Like adults, much of what they achieve is influenced by self-efficacy. Simply put, if children believe they can, they just might, but if they believe they can't, they almost always won't. I guess this is human nature—eventually, you stop trying when you never seem to make the cut.

To what extent were the demands of my profession impacting my wellbeing, or to what extent was the reverse true—was my dubious mental state affecting my decision-making at work? Regardless, red flags took the form of small rebellions as I pushed against the juggernaut the system had become.

I pushed against the absurdity of making a student with additional learning needs struggle through yet another literacy test. I'd enquired about exempting him since we knew, based on the evidence we already had, that he was not yet capable of completing the task as it was designed. I was told that everyone had to do it because we wanted the raw data. I already knew what the raw data would show, and more importantly, so did he.

After twenty torturous minutes, I just couldn't bear to watch it any longer. I told him he didn't need to finish the test because I already knew what great ideas he had. I couldn't put him through another test that would only tell us what we already knew and would be yet another example of what he couldn't do, something of which he was already painfully aware. The teacher aide looked at me questioningly. 'I've just decided he's exempt,' I said.

I felt like I was losing my soul to this corporate model of education that seemed to prioritise ticking bureaucratic boxes and making sure teachers met KPIs. I felt complicit when during the federally mandated NAPLAN (National Assessment Program – Literacy and Numeracy) test, a student leaned across his desk and buried his head in his arms to cry in private. Sitting in a sterile test environment, listening to scripted instructions that made his teacher sound like a robot, my little *thinker* gave up, committing not a single word to paper and gaining a result of zero for the test. His small shoulders shuddered every now and then, giving him away.

It wasn't the first time I'd seen a student fall apart during NAPLAN, but it was one of the turning points in which I seriously questioned whether I wanted to be part of an education system like this. A system that took just forty-two minutes to make a student— and his teacher—feel like a failure.

I quietly removed him from the room and sat with him for a while, steering the conversation away from NAPLAN and toward the excursion we were all looking forward to the following week. His tears dried, and I gave him an early mark so he could be first in line for the pizzas at the tuckshop. As I watched him walk away to claim his place in the queue that was already forming, I knew I'd have to try very hard to convince him he could reach his stars, if I could convince him to look up at all.

How many more tests could the system demand? I wondered. We tested, collated, analysed, and built data walls, sticking up results charts in the staffroom that looked impressive but didn't necessarily capture what the students could do. Whenever I walked past those data walls, I thought about how I used to measure my children's height each year on cute giraffe charts stuck to their bedroom walls. Measuring them more often didn't help them to grow taller. Sometimes I wasn't even sure what we were measuring anymore. I felt too far removed from what I wanted to be—a teacher who knew my students better than their test results.

Increasingly, I felt suffocated by the straitjacket teaching the curriculum demanded, disheartened by a system where, as students moved closer towards their senior years, the end game was to become test savvy so they could pass what they needed to and get out of there. I felt caught in a cycle of over-testing and under-teaching, which was eroding my love of the job and, I feared, my students' love of learning.

By contrast, the student-led climate change protests that would soon galvanise our youth and sweep across many parts of the world would be a living example of the way young people jump into learning what they see as relevant. As a teacher, I'd bet students everywhere during this time held debates, made speeches, and investigated the impacts of climate change. They would have engaged in rich discussion and arrived at their own evidence-backed conclusions. Some would no doubt have uncovered specific areas of interest, like the links between climate change and the devastating bushfires that swept across the country in the same year, thereby becoming experts in their field of enquiry.

Colourful self-made posters proclaimed their energy and commitment. One of my favourites showed the face of Leonardo DiCaprio alongside a burning planet earth and was captioned, *Spot the difference—there is none, they're both too hot.* Their banners were thoughtful and witty, and not only were the teenagers interviewed during the protests articulate and passionate speakers, but they also knew what they were talking about. Our classrooms streamed into the streets as our children made noise and took an interest in a future they wanted to work towards. Here they were, constructively buying into a cause that sparked their social consciousness and about which many were now educating their parents.

The increasing demands on the curriculum, driven by wider societal needs, which by osmosis permeate school life, constitute the 'work intensification' as it was referred to in previous union-led enterprise bargaining attempts. It is an intangible and faceless phenomenon, so I didn't recognise it straight up, but I felt the malignant impact of 'job creep' in my stress levels.

The fact that job creep, sometimes termed 'work creep', has a defined meaning indicates that others have felt it too. Occupational psychologist and author Michael Wellin describes it in the following way:

> Job creep involves ongoing pressure on employees to deliver more than the normal requirements of their jobs ... the employer is gradually increasing their requirements from employees. Behaviour and performance that was previously discretionary now becomes increasingly expected or is taken for granted by the employer.[16]

Job creep is aptly named. The intensity of the workplace crept in so sneakily that I didn't notice. I just became caught up in the ever-increasing email traffic, more testing, more data collection, more need to prove I was doing the 'more' that needed to be done. More scrutiny, more meetings, more demands on reporting, more accountability, more requests for 'honorary and voluntary' participation. More, more, more.

In my early years of teaching, I confused good work with more work. I assumed the more material I had ready to hand out to students, the better I was preparing them. If, for example, we were learning how to write a newspaper article, I collected volumes of articles to dissect in class. We pored over handouts with titles like *The Five W's of a News Article,* and we watched *Behind the News*— news presented in a kid-friendly format.

I gave them comprehension exercises and ran drills on fact versus opinion. When we were so over news articles that we wanted to use them as paper mâché, I brought in more, with increasing levels of complexity that they just didn't need. Naively, I thought I was being a good teacher and congratulated myself on how well prepared they were. I figured they couldn't possibly not understand the task because we'd studied it in so much detail.

Inevitably, the class fell into three general groups. A select few hung in there for the long haul, compliantly reading everything I put in front of them. They were the polite, often passive learners who would be successful no matter what and sometimes—despite what I put in front of them—because of their work ethic.

The second and largest group were students who made creditable attempts to keep up with the workload at first but gave up part way through and simply stopped reading the material I provided. When it came time to write their own, they grabbed at what they could remember in a largely ad hoc way and, for the most part, achieved moderate success.

The third group, not the majority but a significant number, became overwhelmed and struggled to write their own news articles, paralysed by information overload.

A few years into my career, I worked out that when students say they 'don't get it', they often mean they're overwhelmed with too much information and need help to simplify the material in front of them. I worked out, not quickly enough for my earliest classes, that helping kids understand concepts is about clearing the clutter. Filtering out what they don't need so they can focus on what's helpful. It's often about taking away rather than adding to. Teachers who do this are often the ones they will describe as being 'good' teachers because they can make complex tasks seem simple.

When something isn't working in our classrooms, when academic scores are declining, we can make the mistake of assuming we haven't done enough. We try to do better by adding more. We throw more theory into the mix; we add more examples, we hold more tests, we do practice tests to prepare for the real tests, we measure more data, and then we have more meetings to analyse the data. In doing so, we create a point of saturation where people struggle to synthesise the tsunami of new initiatives coming at them.

Just like in the classroom, they either stop listening, grab at things in an ad hoc way, and achieve mediocre success, or they become so overwhelmed they fall back on what they know. Instead, we would be better off asking what needs to be taken out, reduced, simplified to allow us to focus on what's important and effective.

In an attempt to deal with workplace stress, some schools are establishing wellbeing committees. These often function in a voluntary capacity by staff who meet during lunchtime to consider opportunities to promote staff wellbeing. There is little, if any, funding or resourcing for such committees. Some have been able to secure subsidised yoga or meditation classes; others put on special morning teas as a way of getting colleagues together—those who aren't on yard duty, of course.

While these speak to an awareness of the impact of workplace stress and fatigue, without funding and adequate support processes in place, they are usually not sustainable and, in my experience, have only had moderate success. Monday morning teas, while well-intentioned, don't alleviate the impact of increased work demands. More helpful for me was making sustainable tweaks to the way I engaged with work and a clearer demarcation of home and work boundaries. I've become much better at accepting I won't get to every task, every day, and choosing what I spend time on. The best way I can advocate for students is by prioritising the tasks that directly impact their learning. I believe that is what they—and their parents—would want me to do, and I hope it makes me a better teacher, albeit one who doesn't always meet bureaucratic deadlines.

I defy any workplace to beat the education sector for the number of meetings that occur in a school year: staff meetings, morning briefings, subject meetings, year-level meetings, committee meetings. We meet to moderate work standards and calibrate marking. Many occur before or after school or frantically during recess or lunchtime, often with key personnel missing because of other commitments like yard duty or sports training.

Long, professional development sessions held after school and dubbed 'Twilight Meetings' found me sitting at the back of the room looking at the wooden cross hanging from the wall and wondering what would happen if I just climbed right on up there and nailed myself to it. A twilight martyr.

Attendance at twilights was compulsory, and missing them meant having to make up the time later. This was problematic when our children were little because if James was interstate, it usually meant leaving the kids at home on their own. One session had me fidgeting anxiously in my seat as the clock ticked toward 8 pm and it got dark outside. I found it hard to concentrate during the last hour, and the facilitator's voice became a droning reminder that I wasn't where I felt I should be—at home getting my kids ready for bed.

As the demands and speed of school life increased, I felt overwhelmed and unable to keep up, scrambling from one event or lesson or meeting to another. I began ignoring the rules I didn't agree with or openly breaking them. Admittedly, my going rogue wasn't on a WikiLeaks scale but was more along the lines of ignoring the 'No hat, no play' rule, which sometimes saw seventeen-year-olds, less than a year away from voting age, removed from the yard because they were sitting in the sun without a hat. They'd roll their eyes as if to say, 'This is bloody ridiculous,' and I nodded sympathetically, knowing that sun exposure was part of a risk assessment filed somewhere and putting them there mitigated our risk of future litigation. Many of them knew this too.

'Yeah, we know. Our parents might sue the school if we get skin cancer,' they'd say and sit with their arms folded until the bell went to signal the end of lunch.

When a group of senior girls tried desperately to dodge high jump at the athletics carnival, instead of good-humouredly cajoling them to have a go, I gave them all my intel on how to effectively get away with appearing to participate in field events. They delighted in my civil disobedience, and I became the coolest teacher ever.

I baulked at a flowchart the students were supposed to follow when requesting a deadline extension because it required twelve-year-olds to submit a formal application indicating an issue date, a submission date, a reason for the request, and evidence of work completed so far. This was then submitted to the Head of Faculty for approval, after which three copies needed to be filed by different personnel and one retained by the student. Given the high correlation between disorganisation and missing deadlines, I felt the last step was overly optimistic. What happened to simply having a conversation with your teacher?

I brazenly broke the rules I didn't agree with, knowing this may well get me into strife. While once upon a time I would have instigated a conversation around the merits of some of the decisions we made and the impact of those decisions on students, I simply didn't have the ability to articulate my thoughts coherently or the emotional energy to garner the sway I might need to enact change. Instead of jumping through hoops, I simply walked around them. Looking back with a clearer mind now, I think the judgements I made were the right ones. But here's the problem—a big problem summed up in a simple question—what if they weren't?

It's simply not possible for organisations to function effectively if people ignore or break the rules they don't agree with. This is particularly true of schools that depend on high compliance rates to maintain harmony and social order. Despite feeling that too many of our policies were developed without due consideration for individual circumstances, I still felt uncomfortable ignoring and openly breaking the policies and expectations laid down by my employer. I knew that when children are confused with mixed messages—when some teachers say one thing and others say something different—the inconsistency blurs the boundaries and makes school life harder for them to navigate. Just as it has never been important for me to be the 'fun' parent, it was never important for me to be the 'cool' teacher.

Greater demands on our time and increased work pressure are not limited to the education sector. Job intensification permeates workplaces across the country and impacts our mental health as employers, and health professionals alike grapple with the social and economic costs of stress, burnout, anxiety, and fatigue in the workforce. The economic and cultural impact on workplaces when people are not 'in the stadium' but sitting mentally outside it, as I was, are significant. The Productivity Commission report released by the government in November 2020 puts the economic impact of mental illness in this country at 220 billion dollars annually,[17] illustrating the urgent need for reform.

Responding effectively to mental health issues in the workplace demands a sophisticated skill set, well-defined support processes, and a culture of tolerance. This is because episodes are complex and unpredictable, vulnerable to changing environmental stressors, and not finite in their duration. Many times, I was there physically, but my symptoms simmered, escalated, and spiralled without warning. These fluctuations are tricky not only for the person experiencing them but also for our colleagues who have to respond to them because nobody works in isolation. An inhibitor for me was not knowing how long the effects of an episode would linger.

I don't know whether my performance in the classroom operated at a high enough level or my colleagues were giving me space at this time, but I was never called in for a candid conversation. If anything, my colleagues commented occasionally about how calm I was in the classroom. I've never been a shouter, and perhaps because of this, children, including my own, know the amber light, the proceed with caution signal, is activated by a lower-than-usual tone of voice. It's the words not said, the quiet waiting to hear what will come next, that pulls them up.

One of the very first tricks of the teaching trade is to learn how to get the class's attention by lowering your voice an octave below theirs so they can more easily distinguish it from their own. An octave above has the reverse effect—the class will simply keep raising their voices until eventually, everyone is trying to talk over each other and the teacher needs to yell to be heard.

A wonderful image shared by Australian journalist Peter Greste has stuck with me. When he thanked then-foreign minister Julie Bishop for her role in securing his release from an Egyptian prison, he referred to her diplomatic style as like 'being hugged by the Terminator'.[18] This referred to the contrast of her warm smile and her eyes, which he likened to lasers that can burn holes in people's skulls during diplomatic flashpoints. The ability to shut down disputes with a warning glare is something I've witnessed first-hand within my circle of friends. I've seen grown men stop speaking mid-sentence after being shot a warning look from their wives or girlfriends. Even mothers from school have told me they can feel their teenage daughters' eyes burning into them from behind their backs.

'You wait and see,' said one mum, describing her daughter's moods and warning me what I was in for when Cate hit that age. 'Teenage girls shout at you with their eyes.'

The terminator technique maintains the status quo and keeps classroom disputes to a minimum. A well-aimed, well-timed warning glare is often all it takes to stop kids and, it would seem, world leaders, in their tracks. It's effective, non-invasive, and can wordlessly de-escalate a potentially volatile situation from the other side of the room.

It was only on very rare occasions that students heard me yell, and they were usually shocked into a too-scared-to-move silence that I always regretted. This modus operandi earned me the reputation of being calm and unfrazzled, which was so far from my reality at the time, it seems incredulous.

While I survived the day-to-day demands of classroom teaching, I was incapable of the higher-order skills employers look for and depend on in their staff: discernment, problem-solving, creativity, innovation, risk-taking, collaborating in a meaningful way—these were beyond me. I couldn't see opportunities to improve or develop organisational practice, nor did I have the emotional energy to initiate change. Instead, I resigned myself to the inevitable keyboard decrees that were issued via email and often meant more work at my end. Gradually, I developed a 'Just tell me what you want me to do' approach and a quiet 'Fuck it' mentality. It was easier to just tick the boxes. Easier still to appear to be ticking the boxes.

The ability to navigate change in the workplace and in society in general often finds its way into public discourse. It's easy to accept the dominant narrative that people overall don't deal well with change, but I suspect it's not the change phenomenon people resist—it's the additional meaningless workload that change sometimes brings with it that exacerbates workplace stress and fatigue and can be illustrated in the following example.

When a new software program was rolled out, teachers were advised the old software didn't 'speak' to the new, and so the two systems were incompatible. We were, therefore, required to input data into two different systems—essentially the same data, repeated for every student. Added to this, the faculty I worked in went back to recording paper hardcopies—something the technology was supposed to replace. So, we didn't have less data entry; we had more—three times more. A duplication that was time-consuming and made not one jot of difference to student learning. While this example is perhaps trivial and specific to my own context, similar frustrations exist in every workplace.

I've heard employers use sailing as an analogy for change. They point out that change is here, and we'd better get on board the ship or risk being left behind, but it's in the best interests of employers to captain wisely and carefully, not turning the ship too quickly, and ensuring adequate lifeboats are ready to deploy should their employees get left behind in the wake. Retention rates depend on it. We cannot assume it's only the crew who sometimes feel like they're going under—the captains in our schools come close to drowning under their ever-increasing workloads too.

Most of the principals I've worked with do the best they can to shield staff from additional work demands that seep into schools. After one particularly torturous professional development session, I concurred silently with a principal who shook his head in frustration, saying under his breath, 'There's got to be a better way.'

Theirs is the job of selling change to an overworked, stressed, mentally fatigued, and increasingly fragile workforce. Theirs is the job of facilitating change often imposed on them by incoming governments, funding cuts, societal demands, and restructuring. Within this context, it's not surprising that so many of our school leaders and teachers seek career changes or early retirement, and some of my younger colleagues, new to the profession, take time away to reconsider their options. Like me during that time, some quietly find themselves moving closer and closer toward the outer bleachers of the teaching stadium. It's a shame, really, because young people need their teachers to be in the game with them, boots and all.

CHAPTER 16
FEEDBACK

The end of first term is almost upon us, and we're playing one of our favourite games: Hula-hoop hustle. The fluorescent plastic hula-hoops I bought on sale for three dollars a pop are proving to be an excellent investment, especially with the additional ten-percent discount thrown in when the cashier realised I was buying a class set.

On hot afternoons, when concentration is low and the students can smell the holidays just around the corner, we take the hoops to the gym for a brain break. They are a versatile and underappreciated piece of sports equipment, lending themselves to all manner of creative pursuits: we throw them high into the air and catch them with our opposite hand; we twirl them around outstretched arms; we play hula-hoop jump rope; and we hula-hoop like maniacs for the championship prize of a chocolate frog for the last person standing.

I can't help laughing as the boys get their wiggle on with narrow hips that just don't seem to swivel the way they want them to. Every so often, someone loses their mind with all the excitement and I throw a hoop to the side, which becomes a designated 'calm' zone for them to sit in for a while.

Their most favourite game—the hustle, is a relay that involves rolling their team's hoop across the gym without it falling over, in which case the team must begin all over again. We are in the grip of an exciting photo finish as two teams run neck and neck to the finish line. One hoop wobbles ominously, and the runner reaches out to get it back on track.

We hear it before we see it—a toneless grey metronome echoing coldly through the gym. The sound is out of place amid the rainbow cadence of children playing.

The kids stop running because something more urgent has their attention, something even more compelling than winning the hustle. As the game slows, eventually stopping altogether, I follow their gazes. A girl has wandered away from the group; a hot-pink hoop lies on the ground to her side. Her small hands grip a metal pole, an unforgiving colonnade that reverberates each time her head smacks against it. And smacks again. And smacks again. It's a sickening sound, a steady, rhythmic thud that cracks through the stares of children, hushed now by stunned indecision. They look first at their friend, and then at me. Her head *crunches, crunches, crunches,* and things move in slow motion. Although I run, I can't get to her fast enough. Each blow shoots through me like a gunshot.

****

As someone responsible for the education and wellbeing of children all my adult life, their pain became my feedback. Teachers have long been aware that mental health issues among young people are on the rise. The lens of social debate quickly turns to what schools can do to respond to depression, anxiety, eating disorders, self-harm, obsessive compulsive disorders, impulsivity, anger management, and gaming addictions—all of which are evident in our classrooms.

To name these problems by their labels doesn't capture the reality of holding a trembling child whose anxiety digs its way in like a tick. It doesn't capture the desperation of restraining children who throw themselves against a wall or punch themselves with angry fists. Nor the ones who bring lighters or matches to school to burn themselves, such is their self-loathing. It doesn't capture the frantic scene of holding an hysterical child out of harm's way until their distress gives way to physical exhaustion.

How could I find the right words to explain to a distraught parent that their child's injuries are self-inflicted? What's the right answer to give a student who asks to go to the bathroom because they need to purge or cut themselves? How long do I wait for them to return to the classroom before I send someone in to check on them? How do I coax out a high schooler who cowers under their desk to block out the world and its sensory overload? At what point do I evacuate a class because one of their peers is throwing scissors, like daggers, at anyone who crosses their path? How fast do I have to run to stop the sickening sound of echoing metal as a child bangs their head against a pole?

Accessing the right medical help, obtaining an accurate diagnosis, and trialling appropriate medications takes time. The side effects for some of the children in my classes include not being able to eat because the prescribed medication makes them feel sick. Some can't sleep, and for others, it's all they want to do. Some parents make the choice not to medicate their children, especially if they are very young, because of these side effects. Our mental health specialists play a vital role in a health system that can be both complex and costly. A system even less accessible for those living in regional or remote areas or for minority families whose first language is not English.

Australia's mental health system does not focus on prevention and early intervention, and, as stated in the Productivity Commission Report: 'Treatment for many comes too late.'[2] In my experience as a pastoral supervisor, it was apparent that external mental health care providers are stretched to the limit. They triaged, taking on only the most serious cases, if any at all. Even then, by the time they were picked up, many had been left for far too long.

Round-table meetings with our local provider to obtain support for at-risk students became just that—meetings that amounted to little more than discussion because they were at capacity and couldn't take on any more cases.

Accessing professional and affordable mental health support for children isn't easy, with parents frustrated by long waiting lists. Some can't get past the receptionist because clinics are at capacity and not taking on new patients. Of six practices in my local area, none could see new clients within the month, three were not taking new patients at all, and one had an eight-month waiting list. Families in crisis can't hold on for that long. For children who experience hallucinations, hear voices, battle night terrors, or struggle to get out of the house in the morning due to anxiety or OCD, it becomes less about staying plugged in at school and more about staying plugged in to life.

In the interim, many parents seek help through the school, where they can at least speak to a school counsellor, or a teacher who has a vested interest in their child's wellbeing and who often knows them better than most other adults in their life.

The emotional trauma experienced by families unable to get help for a child causes long-term damage, as it did with my friend Jane*, who was trying her best to raise two boys on her own. Her attempts to take away her son's phone led to a physical altercation that ended with her 'falling' against a kitchen cupboard, the handle of which left a nasty gash in her arm. Jane was not only becoming frightened of her own son, she was also desperate to manage the gaming addiction that was turning her child into a stranger. Grabbing tearfully at my tissue box, she explained her reticence to tell anyone, because she didn't want her son to be perceived as violent and out of control.

I'd heard Jane's story repeated by other parents of teenagers who were struggling with gaming addiction. Many were wary about taking away their children's devices, fearing an escalation of the explosive arguments they were having at home. Having received a few warning growls from students myself, I could picture how these scenes unfolded. Family violence of this nature, which is often witnessed by younger siblings, can be isolating because parents see their children's addiction as a parenting failure and blame themselves. They feel it's their fault the situation is so bad and remonstrate that they should 'never have allowed it to get this out of hand'. In listening to their stories, it became clear that gaming addiction among young people is taking a toll on parents.

As was the case in Jane's story, the children themselves are usually engulfed in guilt and feel helpless to change behaviour about which they feel deeply ashamed. In my observation, violent and addictive behaviours can spiral if left unchecked, and the lack of robust and timely support services for schools and families to address the increasing mental health needs of our young people is fertile ground for social disorder to spill over into all aspects of life.

Antisocial and criminal activity in the community is reflected in menacing behaviours, which cross a line in terms of what is considered normal or socially acceptable. These behaviours are felt in our classrooms and have a wide-reaching impact.

Within a school setting, it's the teacher's job to manage and minimise the influence of students who lack empathy or appear to show a lack of remorse. In my opinion, students who are highly manipulative (beyond what is considered normal for the teenage years), who display controlling behaviours or isolate themselves from their peers, children who lie habitually or display aberrant behaviour, can have a profound impact on the emotional and psychological wellbeing of those around them.

When an injured bird became a substitute soccer ball for a student who'd stumbled across it in the yard, other children looked on horrified as it was kicked around, its little body broken, its head hanging limply. I happened to be one of the teachers on duty at the time, and a group of breathless students ran over to alert me to what was happening.

'Miss, Miss! Quick!' They pulled at me, jigging up and down as they tried to impart the urgency they felt. The small crowd that had gathered around the corpse parted to allow me access, and when I spoke to the student later about their part in the feathered mess strewn across the asphalt, they simply shrugged and said, 'It woulda died anyway.'

Cruelty like this is rare, and to provide context, I've lost count of the number of times I've fossicked through the photocopy room for empty boxes or pinched old blankets from sick bay to help kids make hospital beds for rescued birds with broken wings. They tenderly keep their patients warm and calm, and although I know their chances of survival are slim, I also know how important it is for the students who find them to try.

In many cases, intervention strategies and pastoral support systems can bring about positive outcomes for children experiencing emotional distress, especially if the values within a child's family, social, and school networks align. However, this is not the case for some, and I have observed students who continue to display maladaptive behaviours despite ongoing intervention and strong family support. The Productivity Commission report describes 'persistent wasteful overlaps and yawning gaps in service provision'[2] for mental health services, and the need to make the social and emotional development of young people a national priority.

In the wake of terrorist activity, there is a role for teachers to play in identifying behaviours that indicate extremist or violent ideologies. A 2016 article in *The Strategist*, the commentary and analysis site of the Australian Strategic Policy Institute, points out that teachers are in a position to notice behavioural changes in students and enhance the effectiveness of counter-radicalisation messaging. The author, Dr

Anthony Bergin, a senior analyst who has written extensively on a wide range of national security issues, observes:

> Teachers are certainly going to have to be trained in recognising early warning signs and ways in which they can reach out to at-risk youth, just as they do now with drug and alcohol abuse, the dangers of paedophilia or mental health.[19]

The early identification of students who fall into these categories is not enough. Early intervention after detecting risk factors is important to prevent the onset of illness or curtail a deterioration in mental health.[2] Accessing effective, affordable, and ongoing psychological support rather than simply nursing these students through the school years is important if there is any real hope of preventing the escalation of such behaviours. With very few exceptions, the desire to promote the wellbeing of the children in our classrooms is in a teacher's DNA. Students engulfed in sadness, despair, frustration, anger, loneliness, and sometimes violence need our time the most. Our work demands that we're well equipped and capable in a practical sense and that our own emotional and mental wellbeing is in good shape so that we can effectively support them.

Similar scenarios to those I've encountered in my workplaces are replicated in schools around the country. The effects of mental illness and the impacts of antisocial behaviours, which become more complicated and disturbing through substance abuse or gaming addictions, are confronting and heartbreaking to watch. Young people with mental health disorders are at school for six hours a day, and along with parents, we do our best to pick up the pieces when things fall apart.

This is all I could do the day I knelt beside a sad, vulnerable little girl, not knowing whether touching her would make things better or worse as I tried to move her out of harm's way. She sat despondently beside me, as fragile as the broken birds we come across in the yard. Mercifully, the horrible clanging that rang in my ears all that afternoon, and which I can still hear when I think of that day, had stopped.

The truth is, I've never felt my failure as a teacher more than when I've witnessed children physically beating, starving, or cutting themselves in an effort to ease their emotional pain. As I gave out Easter eggs and school broke for the holidays, I wondered if I'd let them down somehow. Had I paid enough attention, or had I looked away when they most needed me to see them?

CHAPTER 17

TRUST

Perhaps it was just me, but the weather felt unseasonably warm that year. By April, the Queensland humidity had usually dissipated, pushed aside by crisper days, but to me, the air felt heavy. My world shook like a mirage menacing the road in a baking summer. In a moment of delusion, I'd promised Mum a trip to Noosa for her birthday lunch—just the two of us. That meant I was about to enter a double danger zone: Mum's birthday and the road to Noosa. The notoriously confusing road signs into Noosa Heads point to 'All Other Destinations' except the one you're actually heading for. Siri chimed in as I looped around one of a string of strategically placed roundabouts—which seemed designed to persuade day-trippers to loop back to where they came from. Mum politely paused mid-sentence while Siri told me to 'proceed to the route', which meant she was lost too. By the time we got to Hastings Street, my head hurt.

Thankfully, our beachfront table meant that Mum looked at the view and not at me. We ordered fancy drinks with cherries and pineapple wedges propped on the rim, and I took my place in a Golden Circle ad of sunshine and sugary smiles. Just like me, my guava, lychee, and coconut water mocktail pretended to be something it wasn't, and I sucked disappointment through a straw.

Still hiding from conversations that might risk exposing the cracks, I was wary because mothers intuitively know when you're not 'right'. Mum ordered her favourite, a prawn and lettuce sandwich, and we chatted about her friends. She gave me a rundown on who was well and who wasn't and her plans to visit my sister in Adelaide. She asked me about a trip I had coming up, and I filled her in on my plans. Safe so far.

After lunch, we browsed in chic boutiques, bustling as usual with the international jet set—big spenders targeted by successful marketing. They mingled with suburban beach kids, identifiable by their sun-streaked hair, denim shorts, and bare feet. I separated the jet setters from the locals by the smell of their sunscreen—coconut oil for the tourists and SPF50 for the locals who knew better. The smell of wooden artefacts, paper flowers, and sandalwood soaps lured us into an eclectic shop full of art and crafts made by local artisans. As I browsed, I found a greeting card by Australian cartoonist Michael Leunig. Looking back at me, a simple, serene fellow sat on a fence and let his feet dangle. He held his own hand, clasped in his lap, and trusted his own company. He waited, despite not knowing what he was waiting for, his head inclined toward the empty space, open to whatever that may bring. He was alone, but not alone. He sat together with himself. There was self-acceptance there.

I placed the card on my bedside table, and it was the first and last thing I looked at each day. The power was in its simplicity. There was something new for me there, permission to rest and greet my own fear. Up until that point, I'd seen it as an enemy, and the battle was wearing me out. Now, I gave myself permission to sit within the space and accept what was happening didn't make sense to me. In this simple card, I somehow felt less lonely and less inclined to fight with myself. I found it comforting that Leunig's fellow was his own best friend.

Something strange started to happen as I set about befriending myself again. I sensed a subtle shift as I learned to be more attentive to a different, more fragile me. If there was something to like in the chap who sat patiently on the fence and trusted himself, then maybe there would be something to like about the new part of me that was emerging. I listened more carefully and checked in with myself often. Some days I did a self-audit on the hour. This was one of the helpful tips I'd found on a mental health app I'd downloaded on my phone. On others, I got to the end of the day and realised I hadn't needed to. This always made me smile in gentle recognition of a small win.

Once I learned how to do them, self-audits became habitual. I regularly stopped to gauge whether my thoughts were racing to out-think each other, loudly jostling for position, or whether they were more ordered, disciplined, willing to wait and take their turn. Some days, my self-talk was highly critical; on others, I acknowledged my successes. I see-sawed between laughing at myself and being weighed down with a stifling intensity. Some days, I challenged myself to take risks, and on others, I steadfastly kept my head down, avoiding the shrapnel that life and work threw my way.

Children in my classes often describe a 'yucky' feeling in their stomachs when things aren't right with them. Depending on the situation, it can be a mixture of sadness, guilt, anxiety, or remorse. They write about feeling 'noreshis', 'nervorce' and wanting to 'vomert'. In these instances, they'll ask to go to sick bay. I have no doubt their emotional turmoil presents as a physical manifestation, and I talk with them about how our bodies are good at letting us know when we need to deal with something going on. I've observed that children who learn to listen and pay attention to their discomfort rather than pushing it away become better at navigating the obstacles in their lives.

It was so easy to dish up advice, and teachers tend to do a lot of it, wanted or not. Next to my bed, the simple, humble fellow who sat with himself on the fence reminded me that creating time and space to take my own advice was fundamental to my wellbeing. Like

I'd advised the students, I paid closer attention to what my body was telling me.

Sometimes I was antsy and couldn't sit still, so I went for long walks along the beach. At other times, I needed the opposite—a quiet corner somewhere calm. The distraction of reading a book, baking a familiar recipe, or flicking through a magazine helped to quieten my thoughts when my brain was swamped with fog, making it impossible for me to process information and make good, timely decisions. On those days, I acknowledged the creeping nervousness within me by gently putting my hand on my stomach to steady the nausea. This didn't make the nausea go away, but in acknowledging it, I had something to work with.

These twenty-second check-ins helped me respond more effectively to the challenges that came my way each day. They helped me choose my battles wisely and pace myself throughout the day so I was more careful about what, and how much, I attempted to take on. I paid attention to how high I was registering on the yuck-scale.

I also practised time-mapping, another tip I'd learned about by scrolling. This involved mapping my day to identify peak times of anguish. For me, the early hours of the morning and the hour or so before bedtime were problematic. This is because my fears percolated in the yawning silence of dawn. I didn't like the ethereal nature of the night either, and no matter what time I went to bed, long, dark hours stretched into a sleepless void. These were the times when the whole world seemed to rest, and I cut a lonely figure wandering through the house, filling in the hours until the family began to stir.

Mapping these times helped me anticipate and prepare for the loneliness and fear that often came then. I made a warm drink, lit a scented candle, or snuggled into my dressing gown—comforted by the soft texture against my skin—and ventured outside to breathe the night air. I gradually became better acquainted with nocturnal life and always had the moon and a possum who'd taken up residence in one of the trees for company.

At school, when I felt my anxiety escalating, I used a countdown method to distract me. I focused on five things I could see: a clock, a coffee cup, a jacket thrown across the back of a chair, a computer screen, a poster. Then four things I could feel: my wedding ring, a breeze coming through an open window, the shape of the mug I held in my hands, a blister forming on my heel. Three things I could hear: the muffled *fupala, fupala, fupala* of the photocopier, the clicking of a keyboard, and always, always the crows. Two things I could smell: fertiliser on the oval and onions frying in the tuckshop. One thing I could taste—the water from my drink bottle. As I practised this technique, it sometimes prevented irrational thoughts from taking hold too strongly.

My feelings of anxiety were often born from a baseless fear, so some days there was little I could do except wait it out. But waiting taught me to listen more intently to my wisdom, and gradually the internal battles became less ferocious. I learned to embrace the days when I needed to sit with myself for a while, dangle my feet over the fence, and hold my own hand. I became better at leaning into the empty space of those days and trusting myself.

CHAPTER 18
UPLIFTED

One of my junior students has lost her library book. It is titled *Frozen*, and she's worried about incurring a penalty. I send an email asking staff to keep an eye out for it in their classrooms. After finding another lost item for a colleague, he thanks me via email and copies everyone in, reminding people to look for 'Sue's frozen book'.

No, I reply to all, *I'm not looking for a frozen book; I'm looking for the book called* Frozen. *But well done for using the apostrophe correctly!* This prompts others to add to the thread—quips about searching in freezers and the need for apostrophes follow. I join in the banter and smile at the trivial nothingness that people make time for. It is strangely uplifting. *Why does this frivolous, uneventful, hardly-worth-mentioning email thread make me feel happy?* I wonder. Is it a small sign, at long last, that I'm opting back in? The irony of the warmth I'd been yearning to feel for so long, and the title of the book that allowed me to feel it, is not lost on me.

CHAPTER 19
LOOKING AT LIFE 'MORE BETTER'

A rock wall neatly frames the grassy hill that stretches along the Mooloolaba esplanade. In summer, young backpackers cook evening barbecues and grey nomads sip wine in fold-out chairs. Families invade the popular picnic spot, their rugs turning the hill into a colourful patchwork quilt, and children sit along the wall kicking their legs as they eat fish and chips out of greasy bags. They lick the salt off their fingers impatiently, eager to go and play. Down on the sand, a game of beach volleyball is underway, and agile twenty-somethings high-five after each point. Sometimes I catch an accent on the wind. *European*, I think. *Perhaps German.*

Many young travellers have made their way to the coast from fruit-picking stints on strawberry farms or orange orchards across Queensland. Some camp out at the beach over the long Australian summer, needing little more than a small campervan with barely enough room to lay a makeshift mattress and a surfboard. They sweep away sea-salt hair from youthful faces or scoop it back into man-buns that some of the boys at school are desperate to grow.

With their own school years behind them, these young travellers collect the world in Instagram pics and friendship bands that decorate deeply tanned wrists. Eventually, as the end-of-summer tides wash in, the accents slow to a trickle and volleyball nets come down in favour of try-lines marked in the sand.

As the locals reclaim the beaches, it sometimes seems as though the backpackers were never there at all, but as seasonal imports, they are a defining feature of coastal life, their energy adding to the summer vibe. It's fun to feel their *joie de vivre* and watch the glow of early summer sunrises through their eyes. It's fun to wonder where they've come from.

****

Unlike many of my friends who backpacked their way around the Continent in their twenties, my first experience of Europe was a school tour of Italy in November 2011. We only just managed to keep a lid on our intrepid band of Aussie teenagers, some of whom had never been on an aeroplane. I was as intoxicated as they were by cobbled streets and hilltop castles, by piazzas, palazzos, and espresso bars. The whole ensemble of Italian life seemed to dance to a never-ending chorale of church bells.

An opportunity to see another slice of Europe came in May 2018, when James and I were able to access accrued long service leave. Knowing a break away from school would help me reset, we considered Greece, which was on our bucket list. While the Italian tour was a true wonder revealed day by day, the responsibility of looking after other people's children, thirty-one of them, meant it was also a lot of work. Greece would be a real holiday with my family after a tough couple of years, and it gave me something to look forward to.

We talked more about the trip; however, the kids' response was lukewarm. Michael was in year eleven and much more settled. He'd taken up surfing as a substitute for cricket and was on track to graduate the following year. Cate was in year nine and making noises about getting a casual job. Our teenage children were at an age where holiday fun looked like weekends with friends and jumping off the rocks at Kondalilla Falls, a popular local swimming hole. They were more interested in surfing at Alexandra Headland and shopping with their friends than ambling around the Acropolis. I tried to bolster their enthusiasm with bribes of souvlaki and baklava from our local markets, but I sensed they were going through the motions to please me. A Greek holiday for a family of four would be very expensive, too expensive if their hearts weren't really in it. As usual, James called it for what it was: our dream, not theirs.

Reluctantly, I swallowed my disappointment and accepted their choice, but I couldn't bring myself to cancel my leave, partly because I didn't want to let go of the dream and partly because I needed a reprieve from work. Rather than shelve the whole trip, James encouraged me to consider doing it without them. We couldn't both go, and while the initial chaos I'd felt in the months following the episode had abated—I wasn't drifting as far or as often—most days, I was just hanging in.

It was indicative of my mental state that travelling solo to the other side of the world, fending for myself in a country I'd never been to, felt easier than fronting up to school. Before COVID-19 stopped the world in its tracks, there were lots of people who travelled alone. But this was a new frontier for me, and given the mental turmoil I'd been dealing with, it was a colossal and perhaps questionable decision.

I knew I would miss James terribly and wished he was coming too. I also knew he'd given me a gift. My being away for almost a month meant he had to step in to cover all things teenager—after-school sport, school runs, homework, part-time jobs—as well as his usual work commitments. My mother-in-law agreed to stay for a few days while James travelled to Sydney on business, and my mum would come around to help with meals and keep an eye on things at home. Trying to ignore the knot in my stomach, I booked through a travel agent who was also a friend of ours. She helped me plan an itinerary and suggested I include breakfast with my accommodation. I felt this was a wise choice, figuring if things turned pear-shaped, I'd at least have a bed and a meal each day.

On my last day of school, a colleague waved and shouted a cheeky goodbye. 'See ya, Shirley!' he called out across the staffroom.

'Ha-ha, very funny,' I called back, wondering if he knew he was about the hundredth person to make the same joke. My friends had jokingly dubbed me 'Shirley Valentine', in reference to the film of the same name in which Julie Walters plays a middle-aged housewife who travels to a Greek island to escape the rut she'd found herself in. One of my colleagues had even asked me if I was running away from something. His question landed a bit too close. I'd been running for nearly two years, and I was so bloody sick of it. I needed to find a way to stop so I could turn and face the world again. My decision to go to Greece was a circuit breaker. It was not only a running-away-from but also a stepping-out-of. I needed to step out of my life for a while to gain a sense of perspective, to help me see more clearly.

It was a brave step for me. Perhaps even a reckless one. Regardless, it was definitely not an easy one, and during the drive to the airport, I questioned whether I was doing the right thing. I'd hugged the kids goodbye at home, knowing that if they waved me off at the airport, I might change my mind and not go at all. James pulled into the drop-off lane and unloaded my suitcase from the boot. I'd asked him not to wait because that would only prolong the apprehension I felt and make saying goodbye harder. I already missed him, and I'd barely got out of the car. But the trip was also a test. If I could manage to get myself across the globe, troubleshoot independently, and survive the unpredictability of a foreign country, then I could survive anywhere, even at home. So, despite my apprehension, I anticipated the challenge too.

Travelling alone meant tackling life differently; it meant consciously taking note of where I was so I could find my way back. It meant stopping to make sense of signs and labels in different languages. Taking each day step by step meant travel by its nature required slowing down and living life more consciously.

I had one night in Athens before leaving on an early ferry to Mykonos. I'd decided not to spend much time on the mainland because the idea of navigating the city on my own was too daunting. This would be something James and I could do together sometime in the future, I reasoned. My accommodation voucher said 'Plaka', which meant nothing to me—I considered my stopover in Athens simply as time to sleep off jet lag and adjust to the different time zone. I took in the city during the taxi ride from the airport to my hotel and tipped the driver. His persistent interest in my having left my husband and children at home and coming all the way from Australia on my own set off a pang of homesickness.

As I answered his questions, I heard a bravado in my voice that I didn't feel. It seemed to fool him though, or if it didn't, he was gracious enough not to let on. The hotel was small and modest but clean and comfortable enough. Once I'd checked in, I flopped onto the bed with relief. *So far, so good.*

It was late afternoon, and I was too restless to sleep, so I pulled open the curtains and glimpsed life as it was happening in the city of Athens. As I took it all in, my gaze shifted upwards towards the top of a rocky cliff. The Acropolis! Right outside my window! I reached for my phone and checked Google images to be sure. I guess my reaction was the same as that of someone seeing the Sydney Opera House or the Harbour Bridge for the first time. Or snorkelling on the Great Barrier Reef. Iconic places have a way of revealing themselves knowingly, as though they've found you rather than the other way around. The Acropolis stood in silent wonder at my disbelief and seemed to whisper, 'I've been here all along …'

I made a beeline for the lobby to enquire about getting there. It was only a twenty-minute walk, and, tired as I was, there was no way I could sleep knowing the Acropolis was waiting just outside my window. Taking a steadying breath, I walked boldly out onto the streets of Athens, *all by myself*, and headed for the ancient ruins I'd dreamed of seeing for so long.

On the way, I passed some markets and, after only a few minutes in the Athenian sun, realised I'd need to buy a sunhat. I browsed in front of a small shopfront where a man stood, one foot in the doorway and one in the narrow laneway. 'Welcome in my shop,' he said. 'I have many more designs inside. My wife will help you choose one.'

It wasn't an invitation so much as an instruction. He had the confident manner of a man who is used to people falling into line, and I did as I was told. He gestured me in, and it took several minutes for my eyes to adjust to the cool dimness of a shop chock-full of sun visors, panamas, and 'I heart Greece' boaters.

I chose a cheap billowy straw hat with a wide brim that flopped around my face. I couldn't resist collecting a bit of Greece in friendship bands for the kids too. As I walked out of the shop and past the boss, I asked, 'Do you like my hat?'

'No!' he replied mischievously. 'I have many more expensive ones!'

I stood at the top of the limestone hill and surveyed the Acropolis, a silent citadel that made me feel protected. Sitting in the shadows of the sun-drenched columns, I closed my eyes and listened as the wind blasted its way through the archways, still testing the strength of this ancient testament to human endurance. White stones and limestone rock crunched underfoot as I wandered around the Parthenon. I thought it was fitting that I was drawn to this temple built to honour the goddess Athena, patron of the arts and literature and, given the battles I'd been having with myself, war. There is something about the ancient buildings and monuments in Europe, something about their survival, their very existence, that helps me trust in the inevitability and continuance of time.

The Greek flag flew proudly in the wind, overlooking the narrow streets of the Plaka district and the rooftops of the houses below. As the first hints of jetlag began to take hold, I reluctantly headed back down the hill, weaving my way through colonies of entitled cats on the prowl for leftovers from the restaurants and cafés lining the alleyways. I quickly came to understand that in Greece, cats own the hood. I walked back through the markets, past the hat shop, and slept until it was time for the ferry to carry me across the Aegean.

Greece and her islands held me spellbound for almost a month as I explored villages, got lost on old tracks that led to hidden churches, and drank in the panoramas that materialised around almost every corner. Why was it that I embraced the idea of getting lost on the backtracks of Greece yet was terrified of getting lost at home? I saluted the sun as it winked goodbye to a magical day in its descent over the sea. I never tired of the whitewashed buildings nestled against the cliffs or the paved walkways that welcomed me with doorways framed by bright-pink bougainvillea, each entrance its own work of art.

One morning, the meltemi—the dry, seasonal winds of the Aegean—fanned the familiar smell of freshly washed linen my way. White sheets flapped from windows and across a narrow laneway to dry in the sun. I found it just as reassuring then as I did when I'd obsessively washed the linen at home. I breathed in washing day in the same way others might breathe in freshly brewed coffee or warm pastries straight from the oven. I hovered around shipping ports and fishing boats as they came in with the day's catch and watched as fishermen tended their nets, a nod to the traditions of the past. It seemed that Greece had waited for me, and I immersed myself in her hospitality.

One afternoon, as I wandered through the maze of Mykonos, constructed purposefully to thwart pirate attacks on the Old Town, I stopped to ask directions to the iconic windmills that sat high on the island but which I couldn't see from where I was in the village. Two boys about sixteen years old looked at me momentarily before one made a show of getting up with a huff and pointed to a sign, which showed the image of a windmill underscored with an arrow pointing the way.

'Next time, you look more better,' he scolded, his contempt clear. I nodded and tried to hide my amusement. Even in a thick Greek accent, there was no mistaking teenage sass. I was back in familiar territory.

'Righteo. Fair enough,' I said quickly, making a mental note to check more carefully for signs from here on in. Clearly, the young locals didn't have much time for middle-aged tourists and their dumb questions. If I'd been floating along on a cloud of romanticism, I was reminded that teenagers worldwide can be so … grounding.

Gradually, Greece forced me to look the world in the eye again, to pay attention to the signs, seen and unseen. Being alone required me to navigate my way around, problem-solve and make decisions. I had to ask questions, clarify instructions, engage in conversation with strangers knowing I couldn't rely on someone else to fill in the gaps. And I felt myself grow stronger. I watched, fascinated by the selfie culture in Santorini as glamorous young people posed openly and unashamedly, adding to their social media posts—some of them no doubt the influencers my children talked about.

On Ornos Beach, a young girl from Texas hired the sun-chair next to me and said yes to everything life had to offer: a still-warm doughnut from the bakery across the street, a bubbly pink cocktail, which she drank as if it were a soft drink, a sunset cruise around the island. She was so full of life, and I realised, sitting in her orbit, that

I'd become careful, cautious, guarded in comparison. Things needed to change, and Greece gave me the confidence to start taking the right steps. Although I'd been away for less than a month, I returned from my Grecian adventure feeling brave and better able to take on the things I'd felt slipping away. There was freedom in the anonymity of travel, which was both liberating and empowering. After too long looking inwards, I felt myself beginning to look outwards again, inspired by the view. I came back resolved to see more of what the world has to offer and more determined than ever that my kids see it too. Greece was a gift, and I'll always remember her friendship with fondness and gratitude for reminding me to look at life 'more better'.

****

In the semester following my return, the days at school weren't the minefield they'd been during the worst of my illness, and for the next year and a half, I functioned at a level that got me through most days unscathed. The once robust after-school debriefs, in which I filled James in on the hurly-burly of the day, dwindled to little more than an exchange of pleasantries because my interactions at school had become mostly transactional.

My illness had taken a toll on him too, and as we approached our twentieth wedding anniversary, we talked about the possibility of taking a family gap year. We were surviving, but we were stuck. A complete career break for both of us would buy me time to consider whether I wanted to continue teaching, and it would provide James with an opportunity to refuel. This proved to be a life-changing decision, which propelled us into a year nobody saw coming.

We sold our family home to help fund the year away and took Cate out of school, intending to home school her as we went. Mike would join us in May—he was enjoying his first taste of independence, having graduated, found work, and moved in with a mate on a short-term lease. James took a redundancy package toward the end of 2019, the result of a company restructure, and timely for us. Ironically, we took this as a sign that the stars were aligned, and on 17 January 2020, three of us flew out of Brisbane International Airport toward the global pandemic, which, unbeknownst to us, was about to ravage the world.

We travelled unimpeded for a few weeks before COVID-19 unleashed itself on Europe, largely relying on house-sitting websites where we looked after people's pets in their absence. This enabled us to experience local life instead of hotel-hopping, which was not our preference or in our budget. We walked two golden retrievers through the streets of Brighton in England, or rather, they walked us while their owners played golf in South Africa.

At the end of January, the contrasting moods of Europe carried us from a wintery United Kingdom into a much warmer Portugal, where I sat one morning at a sunny corner table in a small back-street café. It sold a bit of everything—coffee, cigarettes, souvenirs, pastries, and party paraphernalia. Behind the counter was a fully stocked bar. It was as eclectic as its clientele. Above the ice-cream stand, the television played *Got Talent Portugal,* and a banner hung over the bar boasting local brandy, Portugal Macieira.

Inside, locals sat around small round tables drinking their morning coffee, some reading the newspaper, calling out to each other in greeting. Every now and then, the telltale cigarette smoke, which loiters around European cafés, wafted in from outside. It competed with the aroma of what had become my standard breakfast: strong coffee with lashes of whipped cream and chocolate sprinkles, the Algarvian translation of cappuccino. As I sipped my breakfast, I tuned my ear into the sounds of local banter and indulged in people watching, which is especially entertaining when you can't speak the language.

An old man in a red flannelette shirt bent forward, brown skin wrinkled with years of working in the weather. He reached out good-humouredly to his male companion, and I pictured the two of them working side by side in the avocado farms or citrus orchards we'd seen as we drove through Lagos. The lady behind the counter rested her fingers lightly on the arm of her assistant as they gossiped together. An older tradesman, covered in white dust from the construction going on in the street, threw his arm around the shoulder of the young man slouching next to him, possibly his apprentice. There was companionship here, expressed through the universal and still socially acceptable pre-COVID language of touch.

One man was bigger and louder than everyone else. He leaned casually on the bar, his presence taking up more space than he did. He'd started early on the brandy and was animated in his interactions with the local tradesmen, who nodded at him good-naturedly. As he drank, he became louder and bigger, as is the case with some men who drink a lot.

One of the ladies behind the bar shot him a knowing look, which in English probably said, 'Steady on, mate.' I don't think he saw it, or if he did, he ignored it and ordered another. The lady, perhaps the owner, caught my attention, and we exchanged glances. Her look told me with a resigned smile that he was a local she'd put up with for years. When she came over to wipe down my table, she rolled her eyes, tilted her head slightly in the direction of the brandy man, and shrugged. 'What can you do?'

I remember that café as a place where neighbours gather, as a place of local life and something more than acceptance—affection. It was interesting and hospitable, and that's why I chose it. Without knowing a word of Portuguese, I'd read the personalities as they interacted and was reminded that sometimes we don't need words to understand each other. As I walked out of the café and onto the pavement, I vowed to remember that the next time I was in a meeting and too many words were getting in the way. I wondered whether a nip or two of brandy might help too.

We were back in the UK when England went into its first hard lockdown. Prime Minister Boris Johnson was telling everyone to stay home. Except that we didn't have one. The house-sit we'd arranged had fallen through, Airbnbs were closing, and we had only one night left in our London apartment. Faced with the prospect of homelessness and the very real possibility that we might have to sleep in the hire car we'd managed to keep hold of, we headed out of London and crossed a 16th-century bridge into the ancient market town of Tenbury Wells. For the next two months, we took refuge in a wood cabin, hidden in the farmlands of the Teme Valley, isolated from the 3,777 other people who lived in the village.

We learned to adjust to a different reality in the same way everyone else did—day by day. Gradually, life took on a new rhythm, and I found my footing in a world that had changed with dizzying speed. Road noise was replaced by gusts of wind, which whipped across lonely country tracks and rippled the lake outside our cabin. Instead of shutting the window against the icy wind that blew most days, I invited it in, grateful for the fresh air.

As life slowed down, the streets around us with names like Apple Tree Walk and Old Wood Road fell silent, as if they too were stuck in time. This was a stark contrast to the days when the world moved so fast I had to run to keep up. During the days of lockdown, we sometimes lapsed into companionable silence as we learned a new way to be together in close and continuous proximity.

Perhaps because the mood reminded me of a state of mind I sometimes slipped into, although less often now, I was drawn to the allure of a still, haunting afternoon on a cold beach in the north of England. The piercing call of a lone seagull echoed high above as I walked along a desolate pier. In the distance, two young boys pulled wheelies on their bikes, balancing on their back wheels, expertly dodging clumps of discarded bait and rusted hooks entangled in fishing line.

As the horizon disappeared into a soupy fog, I slipped my hands into woollen gloves and sat to rest awhile like the old wooden boats, which lay tilted on their sides, abandoned by the outgoing tide. They were scattered unobtrusively over the shore, leaning into the emptiness of a cold winter day in the same way that I was learning to do.

CHAPTER 20
FINDING MY VOICE

Early on a cold afternoon in Glencoe, a village in the Scottish Highlands, a white mist hovers reluctantly, holding out against a rising sun. In Scotland, even in summer, the sun rises idly, nudging dreary clouds that dawdle indifferently. It is not the blazing golden sun I'm used to, the one to which I will return soon enough, the early riser that, like an impatient child, pulls me out of bed, ready or not.

Today, only time will decide whether it is strong enough to claim its place in a patchy, silver-streaked sky where, like the clan wars of the past, victory is tenuous. The race is not always to the swift. Eventually, nature unveils wild green mountains, rugged, steadfast, and strong, and the grey sky, splintered with shards of daylight, beckons them upwards.

As I stand in the monolithic shadows of these age-old giants, the Three Sisters, the pandemic that chases us through Europe during 2020 reminds me that time is both infinite and promised to no-one. Gradually, time, that old healer, fades the vast fog of my own fear, and I stand stronger, beckoned by life and welcoming more moments of clarity. Through shards of sunlight, I take a step back into the world I've been hiding from.

****

Almost half of all Australian adults meet the criteria for mental illness at some point in their lives.[2] And one million people with mental illness have never accessed mental health services or seen their GP about their condition.[2] When I was sick, courage spoke to me through other people's stories given a platform during Mental Health Awareness Week and R U OK Day.

I walked past the phone numbers that beckoned from Beyond Blue posters in my local shopping centre and ignored Lifeline, which was only a phone call away. Instead, I listened closely, and still do, to talkback radio when they discussed the topic of mental health. I hung on to every word, hoping to hear something that might help me understand what happened to me. Three people knew—my husband, the doctor he took me to see the day after my mind reached melting point on the motorway, and the assistant principal he phoned to say that I wasn't coming in to work.

In truth, I duped the GP and didn't go back when I didn't get better. While the assistant principal knew I was 'unwell' and 'upset', he didn't know the extent of my condition. The voices, the imaginings, the crippling fear, the paranoia that had overtaken me remained firmly hidden despite the effort it took to keep them locked away out of sight.

Text messages, smiling emojis, and cute dancing gifs disguised the truth with remarkable effectiveness. There were days when I couldn't believe that I was still interacting with people and yet could duck and dodge so that even my family and closest friends didn't know I was sick. This realisation led me to wonder whether the reverse could also be true—how many of my friends, my colleagues, dads at weekend sport, mums at school drop-off, the people from whom I ordered my morning coffee were keeping similar secrets?

On the face of it, seeking help should have been easy. Teachers can access free over-the-phone counselling services, and we had two school counsellors on campus, both women I respected. I'd liaised with mental health providers but didn't access any of these services. Instead, my response was to withdraw, to try and make sense of what was going on, to self-manage, which I largely did in isolation.

In the broader conversation about mental health, I listened to many people, some with high public profiles, speak bravely about their own experiences in interviews and on podcasts. Many other people were dealing with disorders like anxiety, depression, panic attacks, burnout, PTSD, and bipolar disorder; their stories offered a personal dimension that I combined with my practical training and my reading about mental illness to help my recovery. The public discussion was critical in helping me frame my own experience during this time.

As I felt the fog lifting, which happened in much the same way as the mist lifted from the mountains in Glencoe—gradually, hovering at times, clouding over occasionally but lifting nonetheless—I tried to understand why, for so long, I hid in the very shadows that fed my unease. They cast a darkness over my life, which at times was dangerous, but paradoxically, they also shielded me from the light that would expose my truth. I felt simultaneously threatened and protected by them. To understand what happened to me, I reconstructed my illness in a more tangible way. This was my teacher training at work, now an almost involuntary default after years in the classroom. As an English teacher, I witness stories of endurance, courage, and perseverance that unfold in my classroom every day. Time and time again, I've seen the power of storytelling, which has captured human experience since the beginnings of life itself. I reconstructed my illness like a story, and in my head, it goes like this:

I am hiking along a mountain path with a group of friends. The air is cool, and I walk along breathing in the crisp, fresh air without noticing it, because why would I? Why would I notice something as ordinary as air? I've hiked this path before, and I walk with the abandon of my pre-episode self, at peace, oblivious to what life is like when your mind snaps.

I like seeing myself at this point in the story because I don't yet know about the chaos of thought voices. Soon, I will, and once you know something, you can't un-know it. Once you feel something, you can't un-feel it.

Some of the group are slightly ahead, some languish a little behind, and I can hear their voices rise and fall on the breeze. I walk with easy intent, joining in the conversation at times and at others, content to listen to the talk, punctuated by the preening or scratching of birds, who call to each other in birdsong. I'm absentmindedly aware of these sounds, a kind of background bush music that you only notice if it stops.

Suddenly, I misstep and find myself scrambling over the edge of a cliff I hadn't realised was there. Time is suspended as I'm flung around, disoriented in the fall. When I eventually come to a stop, the world is different. Gone is the familiar hiking path, and in its place is rocky terrain I don't recognise. The voices of a moment ago echo now, from … where? I've lost all sense of direction.

There is no fear yet, just a momentary dazed confusion as my mind races to catch up with what's happened. The ground has spun out from underneath me, and as I look around, desperately trying to find my bearings, I realise that in the fall, I've managed to clutch at a ridge. I cling to it, knowing my only choice is to keep my grip and breathe. My legs dangle into a great void below.

And when I'm at my most vulnerable, Fear finds me. It brings foreboding and delivers a punch, stealing my oxygen like the thief it is. It is infinite and comes in the form of dark, swirling circles that gurgle ominously. It has the power to send me falling into the abyss below, silently, so nobody would even notice until they looked up one day to find me gone. I dare not look down. In the seconds that follow, I close my eyes and focus only on breathing because breathing means I'm still alive.

When I do look up, I see blurry figures looking for me. They are close enough to hear me cry out, but in my terror, I can't speak. All my physical and mental energy goes into holding on. I hang there for as long as my strength holds out because reaching out means letting go of my grip. It means risking a possible freefall into nothingness. The thought of the fall is paralysing, and faced with the choice, holding on feels safer. While I'm holding on, I'm still here.

I don't have the courage to loosen my hold, to reach for hands that might be able to get me, if not all the way back up, at least closer to the path. What if they miss? What if I miss? I dangle over the edge, holding on for nearly four years. I guess this takes a different kind of strength. I build up my emotional muscles, and I find other ways to climb out: little crevices I hadn't seen in my panic, small footholds that guide me back towards the path I fell from. Each time I find one, I learn more about myself, my ability to survive, to find my way back. I get better at finding signposts, which help guide me.

While I dangle there, I learn more about Fear. It's a terrible tormentor, a silent, menacing stalker that meanders through my life and, at times, robs me of it. I see it, I feel it, and at first, I waste too much energy kicking it away.

Gradually, we become better acquainted, and I come to think of it as just that—an acquaintance. No bigger or stronger than Loneliness, Peace, Anger, Joy, or Sorrow. We are not friends, but we are not enemies anymore. When our paths cross, I need to acknowledge it before it will let me pass. Sometimes I have to give it a bit of a push, but I don't wrestle or fight with it the way I did before. Nor do I run, because it chases me when I do, and I now understand that running is futile. As with all bullies, it is better to turn and face it, and each time I do, Fear loses its control over me. Slowly, I find my voice again and take back the ability to live the life I want.

When I eventually find my way back to the path, one I know I may never tread in quite the same way again, James is there, waiting. I'm sure he's been tempted to simply climb down and carry me back up, but I'm glad he doesn't because then I would learn more about my weakness than my strength. It is in the climb that my emotional endurance grows stronger. Instead, he watches, guiding me occasionally, and waits for me to find my way back. When I have the strength to look outward again, no longer consumed by my internal battles, I realise that four years is a long time for him to watch me dangling, kicking furiously at my fear one moment and paralysed by it the next.

****

On my desk at school sits a sketch of a young American Indian girl whose eyes hold a wisdom belying her age. On the sketch is written: *For the hearts of children are pure, and therefore the Great Spirit may show to them many things which older people miss.* She reminds me never to overlook the wisdom of young people. As I looked at her in my difficulty, I reflected on the brave legacy of Dolly Everett, a teenager from the Northern Territory who tragically succumbed to the pressures of cyberbullying.

Amid Dolly's pain, she encouraged people to 'Speak, even if your voice shakes'. While we battled different enemies, her message was powerful and, inspired by her courage, I tested my voice. For a long time, it didn't just shake; it broke completely, and I choked on the words. Gradually, as I learned to speak in the presence of fear, my internal voices became quieter, and my outside voice shook less.

By the time I could speak again, I'd carried the secret of my illness for a long time. It wasn't a secret I wanted, and because I panicked and hid, pulling the shadows down around me, because I created veils of deception to protect myself, cloaked in pretence and avoidance, my secret became bigger and heavier and harder to tell. While I'd been dangling over the emotional edge for four years, I'd deceived the people I loved and denied them the chance to show the kindness I knew would have been shown in abundance.

I've heard people talk about the stigma of mental health, so I looked up the word 'stigma', which means a stain or a blemish. While I don't feel either of these things, I recognise that I am different to how I used to be. Knowing myself differently makes me stronger. That strength was tested on our start-stop-start-stop trek through Europe, surrounded by the increasing fear and uncertainty that gripped the world during the height of the pandemic.

We had to troubleshoot daily as borders opened and closed according to case numbers, and we needed to constantly evaluate the direction of travel and the length of time we stayed in one place.

The risk of getting stranded because of a swift border closure was an everyday reality, and it reminded me of *Get Smart*, one of my favourite television shows as a kid. In the show, secret operative Maxwell Smart battled the enemy, appropriately named KAOS, whose aim was world domination. The chaos in Europe and the battle for control over the virus, which was doing its best to take over the world, meant no matter which direction we went, borders were only open for a short time before they slammed shut behind us. Just as the doors slammed behind Max as he walked through the corridors of Control Headquarters in the closing credits.

Separated from Michael, who remained in Australia, and not knowing when we'd be able to get home, I braced for another mental collapse. It seemed inevitable when almost every country in the world was counting its dead by the day. Media reports showed desperate governments trying to cope with overwhelmed health systems, constructing makeshift hospitals, and digging mass graves in a bid to cater for the sick and dying that escalated hourly.

The thought crossed my mind that we could end up in one of the hastily constructed Nightingale hospitals in England. They reminded me of the transportables (temporary classrooms) I'd taught in once, little more than dongas fitted for purpose.

Newsfeeds, which had fuelled my earlier paranoia, showed grief and loss on a global scale. Grief, the very thing I'd named as my greatest fear, now crippled the world. Like everyone else, I heard the personal stories of emotional and mental trauma made worse by forced social isolation. Night after night saw us tuned in to press briefings, trying to make sense of graphs that identified virus hot spots, predicted trends, and explained the R-number— the infection rate. As borders went up and Europe shut down in a bid to flatten the curve, I waited for the symptoms of my illness to take over again.

I waited for the voices to return, for the nausea and brain fog and the all-too-familiar disorientation. I anticipated the head shakes and the paranoia, which had emerged when I'd relapsed previously, and the internal battles that would sap my emotional energy and rob me of my memory. Worst of all, the thought of getting in the ring for another bout with Fear filled me with dread. However, for reasons I can only guess at, my mental health held up, and when we flew out of Milan at the end of November 2020 and into Perth to complete hotel quarantine, I was in pretty good shape. Surprisingly good shape, in fact, given that conditions were testing even the most emotionally resilient. The two weeks' enforced isolation, with security guards posted on every floor and without the ability to even open a window, saw James, not me, pacing the floor when the world shrank to the size of our hotel room and restlessness closed in.

Perhaps it was all the practice I'd had with emotional isolation that helped keep my illness at bay. Perhaps it was because I'd learned to recognise and understand uncertainty and was adept at leaning into the empty space of it. Or I remembered the exhausting futility of running from fear and was braver about turning to face it, reminding myself it was no more powerful than peace, joy, sorrow, or anger.

I've never won a trophy for anything in my life, but if there was a Best at Social Distancing prize up for grabs, I would have nominated myself for Player of the Year. Self-imposed isolation was a condition of my illness, which meant I was familiar and well-practised at coping with the social disconnection of lockdowns and mandatory quarantine. When life changed in a way that none of us could have foreseen, I flexed the emotional muscles I'd built up and held on, knowing the uncertainty, the fear, and the loneliness would pass. The year of the pandemic was the ultimate test of my emotional strength.

CHAPTER 21

PEACE

It's early on a summer's morning when I strap Atlantis to the top of the car. I look up into the clear January sky, drinking in the depth of blue nothingness that stretches to every horizon. I breathe in deeply, inhaling the freshness of the early morning, and pause for a moment in its stillness. Like the air and the sky, I am still. It's a moment of peace, and because we are getting reacquainted, I let myself linger and acknowledge the quiet friendship the day offers.

Today, I get straight onto the board and paddle out, leaning into the swell as it lifts me up and over, up and over, finding my balance without effort. I listen to the sound of the water as it laps spasmodically over the board. This time, I peer down, hoping to catch a glimpse of ocean life. Stingrays glide with purpose when I come close, their tails silently betraying them, no longer camouflaged against the sandy bottom of the ocean. Seabirds plunge and dip, looking for food, flying archers with deadly aim. Fish dart away as the shadow of the board blocks the sun. I am here.

Mooloolaba beach beckons me, and I paddle towards it with strong, controlled strokes. I like the sure way the paddle moves through the water, pushing me forward. It's not a weapon this time but a tool I use to maintain my direction and speed. A few metres out from the shoreline, I lay face down on the board and dangle my arms in the water, feeling the flow of the current rush between my fingers. I close my eyes, abandoning myself to the whims of the wind, and feel the power of the Pacific beneath me. It's the closest I can get to hugging the ocean. Gentle swells form a rhythm, and a summer breeze comes and goes. I spend the day in and out of the water according to my own rhythm: paddle, swim, rest—paddle, swim, rest.

As dusk descends, I paddle back in for the last time that day and heave the board up onto the sand. A couple of girls from my junior English class walk past and give me a friendly wave. I smile and wave back before strapping the board back onto the roof of the car, and then wander down to the water's edge for one final look before heading home. A weakening sun still glitters over the ocean, making its way towards night, casting a soft glow over the Spit. The sand cools beneath my feet as it loses the heat from the day. I cast my eye over the long distance I've paddled and nod to the ocean as a gesture of gratitude. It feels good to be back here again.

****

If years of teaching have taught me anything, it's that the power of the human spirit reaches out and touches us in ways we don't anticipate. It touched me at the back of a classroom when a young boy's voice ignited us all, and it was there as I sat beside a sad little girl, knowing how she felt because there were days when I felt broken too. It's in the waiting chairs and the standing ovations and imprints etched on kitchen tables. I see it in the camaraderie of camp groups and hear it in the sounds of school spirit that drift across ovals. And it was all around me when, as a young teacher, I stood as a sad witness on a cold, grey day and cried with a grieving father who would never know I was there. In these raw moments of vulnerability, we are connected most deeply.

I've felt this my entire career working alongside young people, sharing their grief and joy in equal measure. Watching them step courageously through their lives, advocating for them, challenging them, sitting with them as they learn, sometimes brutally, that life isn't always fair. I feel it when they tell me or show me they aren't safe. I see it as they learn to forgive themselves and others, to live their lives with hope and purpose, to own their mistakes, to lobby for the kind of world they want, to move forward into an exciting and ever-changing landscape called the future. I feel it, as I always try to teach with compassion and optimism, modelling truth—*veritas*—in the same way my teachers did. I hear it in spontaneous laughter that ignites a classroom, and I see it as I watch them learn to live in the grey, discovering that we learn more in the questions than the answers. As they tease, joke, bully, and protect each other, each one finds a place in my heart. Our classrooms are places full of unexpected sacred moments born out of the ordinary.

In the early throes of my illness, when I was sickest and on my lowest, darkest days, I knew that if my classroom was compromised, I'd walk away. Despite years of juggling motherhood with working and studying to complete a master's degree, despite all the night, weekend, and holiday hours I'd put in, I found it relatively easy to let go of leadership positions. It was a relief to put distance between myself and the bureaucracies that come with management roles I was never completely invested in anyway—not in the same way I was invested in the classroom. Resigning from these positions was a matter of my survival.

Perhaps it's human nature to look for someone or something to blame when our lives fall apart. I looked around and saw teaching and became increasingly angry and frustrated at a system that I blamed for making me sick. I resented the workload, the pressure, and the accusations that schools are letting kids down. I bought into parents' angry outbursts, overlooking the fact that these often stemmed from financial worry, exhaustion, or the guilt and stress of a marriage breakdown. I railed against a system that measured kids by numbers and seemed hell-bent on testing the life out of them. I grew increasingly irked at the 'honorary and voluntary' hours spent away from my family, knowing I would never get that time back with them. I was sick, scared, increasingly isolated, and I blamed teaching. I wanted out.

While James sympathised, he pointed out we still had a mortgage to pay, school fees to cover, and we needed my income. Instead of walking away completely, I reduced my hours, but getting myself to school each day was gruelling. When the bell went to signal the beginning of the school day, I wanted to rip the speakers out of the wall. When the floaty voice on the other end of the PA led us through five minutes of daily mindfulness, I wanted to throw something at it. Inside my head, at the mercy of my thoughts was the last place I wanted to be. I'm ashamed to say that whenever my kids got sick, a part of me hoped they were just sick enough to justify my taking time off work. This made me feel like the worst mother in the world.

If I had sought the professional help I should have, I might have recovered earlier. If I'd been honest and brave enough, I might have found my voice sooner. But it was easier to be angry with teaching, to blame it for my state of mind, the cause of my terrifying fall and my emotional exhaustion from holding on.

Undoubtedly, the demands of teaching have had an impact on me, and all the things I've named are real—the work intensity, the stress, the fatigue, the emotional overload, the frustrations with the system. Yet, in many ways, teaching has been my panacea too. The magic and miracles of the classroom; the ordinary moments that unexpectedly erupt into joyous, raucous standing ovations; kids who find the power of their own voices and jump despite their legs shaking with fear; the ones who wait until dark because they won't give up on a friend; those who gather to finally farewell one of their own. These are the healing, life-giving moments that have shaped my teaching career.

As much as I cursed teaching, resented it, and raised my voice against it, as much as I could feel it sucking the life out of me at times, it also breathed life into me in so many ways. It seized its pound of flesh one day, only to return it in abundance the next. It took me to dark places and then led me back into the light. For a while, I lost myself to teaching, but I found myself again there too. I have been both trapped by the bell and saved by it.

Erin Hanson, an Australian poet, offers this wisdom:

> There is freedom waiting for you,
> On the breezes of the sky,
> And you ask, 'What if I fall?'
> Oh, but my darling,
> What if you fly?

I know there will be times when I fall. But I will fly too.

ABOUT THE AUTHOR

Sue is a high school teacher who entered the noble profession of teaching in the last century. A long-ago time, when text messages were scribbled notes on the ripped corners of lined books that kids *wrote* in. Her crown fell off when a sassy girl in her English class asked, 'Who died and made *you* Queen?' She gathered the remaining shreds of her  dignity and sat on the floor alongside the students—the real princes and princesses in her classroom—and liked it better there.

A storyteller and educator who believes ordinary moments don't exist, her stories have appeared in a range of travel and educational magazines, such as *Education Review*, *Profile Magazine*, *Athens Insider*, and *Italia!* She holds a Bachelor of Education from South Australian College of Advanced Education (Flinders University) and a Master of Educational Leadership from Australian Catholic University. Sue was a finalist in the 2015 Teaching Excellence Awards in Brisbane, but her most highly valued awards are from her students—the heartfelt notes, smiley faces, and dragonfly pictures that adorn her desk.

Sue lives in Queensland with her never-say-no husband and two teenagers who are much better drivers than her.

Email the author at teacherscrytoo@gmail.com.

Contribute to the conversation about teacher wellbeing and mental health in education via Instagram @teacherscrytoo.

Excerpts from *Teachers Cry Too* have been published with permission in Profile Magazine under the title *Stopped in our Tracks*, 30/04/2020, and in Education Review under the title *Reading for fun: the last bastion of the english classroom*, 22/02/2021.

ENDNOTES

1 G Goldberg and R Houser, 'Battling Decision Fatigue', *Edutopia*, George Lucas Educational Foundation, 19 July 2017, viewed 3 Sep 2021, https://www.edutopia.org/blog/battling-decision-fatigue-gravity-goldberg-renee-houser.

2 Productivity Commission 2020, *Mental Health*, Report no. 95, PC 2020, Canberra, viewed 3 Sep 2021, https://www.pc.gov.au/inquiries/completed/mental-health/report/mental-health-volume1.pdf.

3 M Bode, 'Classmate horror as girl falls', *The Courier Mail*, Nationwide News Pty Ltd, 22 Sep 2009, viewed 8 Jan 2021, https://www.couriermail.com.au/news/queensland/sunshine-coast/classmate-horror-as-girl-falls/news-story/a1c6cfa8cde51900ed35aef97c1a8695.

4 D Bathersby, 'School camp fall girl on the mend', *The Courier Mail*, Nationwide News Pty Ltd, 30 Sep 2009, viewed 8 Jan 2021, https://www.couriermail.com.au/news/queensland/sunshine-coast/school-camp-fall-girl-on-the-mend/news-story/41ffe19e8f67b33dd207d205bfaade9a.

5 ABC, 'Tiahleigh Palmer's murder and how the investigation unfolded', *ABC News*, 24 Mar 2016, viewed 20 Jan 2022, https://www.abc.net.au/news/2015-11-13/tiahleigh-palmer-murder-timeline/6926556?nw=0&r=HtmlFragment.

6 *The Final Quarter,* Director Ian Darling, Sydney, NSW, Shark Island Productions, 2019.

7 Mission Australia, *Domestic and Family Vioence statistics,* MA, 2021, viewed 27 Aug 2021, https://www.missionaustralia.com.au/domestic-and-family-violence-statistics.

8 Lifeline, *Resources: Data and Statistics,* n.d., viewed 27 Aug 2021, https://www.lifeline.org.au/resources/data-and-statistics/.

9 TeachThought Staff, 'Teachers: The real masters of multitasking', *Pedagogy,* TeachThought, n.d., viewed 14 Dec 2021, https://www.teachthought.com/pedagogy/teacher-makes-1500-decisions-a-day/.

10 P Stapleton, 'Teachers are more depressed and anxious than the average Australian', *The Conversation,* The Conversation Media Group Ltd, 7 Jun 2019, viewed 31 May 2021, https://theconversation.com/teachers-are-more-depressed-and-anxious-than-the-average-australian-117267.

11 T Moore, 'One in three Australian teachers leaves in first five years, inquiry hears', *Brisbane Times,* 25 Feb 2019, viewed 14 Dec 2021, https://www.brisbanetimes.com.au/national/queensland/one-in-three-australian-teachers-leaves-in-first-five-years-inquiry-hears-20190225-p5106h.html.

12 P Wood, 'Australian school principals attacked and threatened at record levels, report finds', *ABC News,* ABC, 27 Feb 2019, viewed 8 Jan 2021, https://www.abc.net.au/news/2019-02-27/school-principals-attacked-by-students,-parents-says-acu-report/10850336?nw=0&r=HtmlFragment.

13 Dr P Billett et al., *Teacher Targeted Bullying and Harassment by Students and Parents: Report from an Australian Exploratory Survey*, ResearchGate GmbH, Apr 2019, viewed 8 Jan 2021, https://www. researchgate.net/publication/332538760_Teacher_Targeted_ Bullying_and_Harassment_by_Students_and_Parents_Report_ from_an_Australian_Exploratory_Survey_Table_of_contents_ ACKNOWLEDGEMENTS_2_PROJECT_SUMMARY_ AND_KEY_FINDINGS_2_BACKGROUND_3.

14 N Afshariyan, 'Nearly all Australian teachers have been bullied by students and parents', *Triple J Hack*, ABC, 7 May 2019, viewed 8 Jan 2021, https://www.abc.net.au/triplej/programs/hack/australian-teachers-bullied-by-students-and-parents/11085130.

15 H Vnuk, '"Tantrums, swearing, physical abuse": The bullying of teachers by parents has got to stop', *School*, Mamamia, 12 Mar 2019, viewed 28 Aug 2021, https://www.mamamia.com.au/abuse-of-teachers/.

16 M Wellin, *Managing the Psychological Contract: Using the Personal Deal to Increase Business Performance*, Gower Publishing Limited, Hampshire, 2007.

17 S Dalzell and A Henderson, 'Productivity Commission report into effect of mental illness reveals $220 billion annual cost to economy', *ABC News*, ABC, 16 Nov 2020, viewed 30 May 2021, https://www. abc.net.au/news/2020-11-16/productivity-commission-releases-mental-health-report/12887012.

18 J Dye, 'Journalist Peter Greste delivers blunt message to politicians on detention centre secrecy', *The Sydney Morning Herald*, 26 Mar 2015, https://www.smh.com.au/politics/federal/journalist-peter-

greste-delivers-blunt-message-to-politicians-on-detention-centre-secrecy-20150326-1m8dqi.html.

19 A Bergin, 'New measures to counter radicalisation in Australian schools', *The Strategist,* The Australian Strategic Policy Institute Blog, 19 Feb 2016, viewed 29 May 2021, https://www.aspistrategist.org.au/new-measures-to-counter-radicalisation-in-australian-schools/.